Here I Am

Here I Am

How God Reveals Himself in Everything from
Science and Suffering to Birthdays and Baseball

Keith Scott

RESOURCE *Publications* · Eugene, Oregon

HERE I AM
How God Reveals Himself in Everything from Science and Suffering to Birthdays and Baseball

Copyright © 2021 Keith Scott. All rights reserved. Except for brief quotations in critical publications or reviews, no part of this book may be reproduced in any manner without prior written permission from the publisher. Write: Permissions, Wipf and Stock Publishers, 199 W. 8th Ave., Suite 3, Eugene, OR 97401.

Resource Publications
An Imprint of Wipf and Stock Publishers
199 W. 8th Ave., Suite 3
Eugene, OR 97401

www.wipfandstock.com

PAPERBACK ISBN: 978-1-6667-3124-8
HARDCOVER ISBN: 978-1-6667-2354-0
EBOOK ISBN: 978-1-6667-2355-7

10/22/21

Dedicated to George Mitchell, the high school teacher who inspired my lifelong interest in the humanities and who laid the foundation for my faith in God

"Religion and science demand for their foundation faith in God. For the former (religion), God stands foremost; for the latter (science), at the end of all thought."

—Max Planck, physicist, Nobel laureate, and originator of quantum mechanics

Contents

Introduction | ix

I. Him | 1
II. Science | 9
III. Love | 35
IV. Pride | 49
V. Suffering | 72
VI. Gifts | 101
VII. Sabbath | 112

Bibliography | 129

Introduction

The Ultimate Hypothesis

> "Imagination is more important than knowledge. For knowledge is limited, whereas imagination embraces the entire world."—Albert Einstein

What a strange thing for a scientist to say. I was always taught that scientists were more perceptive than imaginative. They tested hypotheses and expressed their findings with mathematical precision. They formulated theories to predict outcomes so mankind can *know*.

It seems like imagination would be the least important faculty for someone whose work was all observations and measurements, tests and outcomes. And yet one of the eminent scientists of all time said that imagination is more important than knowledge.

If using your imagination means conjuring images of unicorns and magic carpets, or believing that you're the King of England and that you walk on three legs, then it would be of no use to a scientist (unless the scientist is a psychologist) and Einstein would've been wrong. The dreams of an innocent child and the delusions of a deranged adult tell us nothing about the world that scientists study.

INTRODUCTION

It must be that Einstein defined imagination differently. I bet he would have said that imagination is more like insight; it's when we observe something that we can't explain, and then imagine what might explain it. It's the mind's effort to expand its reach even if it's not yet able to grasp what it's reaching for.

In other words for the scientist it's a hypothesis—an imagined explanation for facts that can't be explained otherwise.

The ability to imagine a hypothesis is where science begins, and one of the earliest hypotheses nicely illustrates how that's so. Over two thousand years before we could see it with an electron microscope, Democritus imagined the atom. It was invisible to him of course; that's why he named it *atomos,* Greek for invisible. And in a sense all hypotheses imagine things that are invisible, at least when the scientist comes up with the hypothesis.

What else can we imagine that's invisible today but might become visible in the future? It's a tantalizing question, one that should make you curious, but it can also be frustrating; when we imagine a hypothesis and test it, the answers that we get just lead to more questions.

Physicist Niels Bohr may have experienced that frustration. He modeled the atom as a nucleus with orbiting electrons, which was a brilliant insight. But when he tested his hypothesis and the results strongly supported it, another question arose: How did the orbiting electrons avoid the laws of electricity and magnetism under which they should spiral into the nucleus instead of orbiting it? Eventually that question was answered—electrons aren't subject to electrostatic attraction because they're quantized wavefunctions (whatever those are . . .)—but it had to leave Bohr wondering why his insight simultaneously brought him one step closer to, and one step further from, understanding the atom.

It's a challenge scientists face all the time. The poet Edward Young wrote these lines about their predicament: "With endless questions be distressed, all unresolvable, if earth is all."[1] Theologian Thomas Aquinas made the same point. "All the efforts of the human mind," he said, "cannot exhaust the essence of a single

---

1. Young, *The Works,* 187.

fly."[2] And inventor Thomas Edison was even more blunt. "It's obvious," he said, "that we don't know one millionth of one percent about anything."[3]

Einstein would have agreed with all of them. He said mankind's "dull faculties" can only comprehend things "in the most primitive forms."[4] We know that nature operates under certain laws but our "actual knowledge of these laws," Einstein said, "is only imperfect and fragmentary."[5] It's as if there was a jigsaw puzzle with an infinite number of pieces—the endless questions that bedevil scientists—and no matter how many pieces mankind puts together, the whole picture remains elusive.

That scenario can make some people doubt there even is a picture, but not Einstein. He believed that "behind anything that can be experienced there is something that our minds cannot grasp, whose beauty and sublimity reaches us only indirectly."[6] He sensed a "spirit manifest in the laws of the universe," something grand and awesome that caused everything and could explain it all.[7] He said that . . .

> " . . . behind all the discernible laws and connections, there remains something subtle, intangible and inexplicable. Veneration for this force beyond anything that we can comprehend is my religion."[8]

He believed that what's "mysterious" and "impenetrable to us really exists."[9] It was the "source of all true art and science" and showed

2. Aquinas, *The Three Greatest Prayers*, 41.
3. Stevenson, *Quotations*, 1059.
4. Rowe and Schulmann, *Einstein on Politics*, 229–230.
5. Einstein, *Albert Einstein, The Human Side*, 32–33.
6. Isaacson, "Einstein & Faith," para. 25.
7. Einstein, *Albert Einstein, The Human Side*, 32–33.
8. Isaacson, "Einstein & Faith," para. 15.
9. Rowe and Schulmann, *Einstein on Politics*, 229–230.

"itself as the highest wisdom and the most radiant beauty."[10] It made the universe a "miraculous order."[11]

When all of the answers that science provides only lead to more questions, why did he believe that this venerable spirit and force was actually there? "The belief in the existence of basic all-embracing laws in nature," he said, "also rests on a sort of faith."[12]

This is where Einstein's reach exceeded his grasp. He couldn't explain what he could see in his mind's eye but it had enough power and substance that he accepted it on faith.[13]

And so it goes. Writers and painters face a blank tablet or canvas and are inspired by their "muse." Athletes outperform when they're "unconscious" and "in the zone." Lovers delight in "what's between us" or sigh because, like the blues ballad goes, they'd better "let love depart." At one time or another almost everyone senses the presence and influence of a transcendent reality.

For scientists that reality—Einstein's force behind everything that we experience and all of the universe's laws—would be the Ultimate Hypothesis; it would explain . . . everything. And Einstein's faith in its existence motivated him because he knew that each piece of the puzzle that he discovered pointed to something magnificent. The astronomer Johannes Kepler, a leading figure in the seventeenth century's scientific revolution, said as much. By examining the laws of the universe, he said, "we observe to some extent the goodness and wisdom of the Creator."[14] Einstein went even

10. Rowe and Schulmann, *Einstein on Politics*, 229–230.

11. Calaprice, *The Einstein Almanac*, 91.

12. Einstein, *Albert Einstein, The Human Side*, 32–33.

13. Many atheists want to claim Einstein as one of their own, but it's no use. They have to account for his belief based upon what he said and wrote, and the words that he used to describe what he sensed are telling. He wrote of a "spirit" and a "miraculous order," something "intangible" and "inexplicable" that was "behind" the universe. He explicitly rejected atheism and, while he also rejected the God of the Bible, he always retained a faith, vague though it was, in a transcendent being or force. It seems like his god, to borrow from Abraham Lincoln, existed on a "dark indefinite shore." Or to put it more precisely like physicist and Nobel laureate Max Planck, for Einstein the scientist God existed "at the end of all thought."

14. Caspar, *Kepler*, 381.

INTRODUCTION

further. "The cosmic religious experience," he said, "is the strongest and noblest driving force behind scientific research."[15]

"What worries me about religion," atheist Richard Dawkins said, "is that it teaches people to be satisfied with not understanding."[16] He couldn't have been more wrong. Einstein's faith animated his genius and he had some harsh words for the "fanatical atheists" who "cannot hear the music of the spheres."[17] Anyone who "cannot pause to wonder and stand wrapped in awe," he said, "is as good as dead."[18]

The poet Alfred Lord Tennyson said it a little differently. He wrote about our scientific theories or "systems" as he called them, adding a thought about the ultimate mystery behind the universe:

> Our little systems have their day;
>
> They have their day and cease to be:
>
> They are but broken lights of thee,
>
> And thou, O Lord, art more than they.[19]

When I was a young man, I didn't believe in God. If you'd asked me whether God existed, I would have said, simply, "no." The universe was composed of matter and energy and that's all there was to it.

Now I believe otherwise. While atheists disparage believers for taking the Bible too literally, I think they are susceptible to criticism on the same grounds—they take the world too literally. All of the atheists that I know don't just doubt there is a God; they are certain he doesn't exist. They are like the minority of believers who take the Bible so literally that they're sure God created the world in seven twenty-four hour days, or that he commanded us to pluck an eye or yank a tooth from anyone who took an eye or a tooth. When it comes to God these atheists and their foils are more alike than they

---

15. Einstein, *"Religion and Science,"* para. 13.
16. Dawkins, "Heart of the Matter," BBC
17. Jammer, *Einstein and Religion*, 97.
18. Rowe and Schulmann, *Einstein on Politics*, 229–230.
19. Tennyson, *In Memoriam*, lines 17–20.

know. They're both looking at the surface of things and assuming there's nothing left to learn. They have let their curiosity and imagination atrophy. Intellectually, they're "as good as dead."

I've written this book for both believers and atheists. If you believe but feel like you've lost your way, I hope this book will put you on a path back to God. If you don't believe, however, you must let go of your denial before you start reading. I'm not suggesting that you let it go completely, lie to yourself and pretend that you have the faith of a saint. Instead, you should postulate the existence of God like a scientist who formulates a hypothesis to explain facts that current theories fail to satisfactorily explain.

Every era is blind to its own prejudices and ours is no exception; we assume that faith and reason are necessarily at odds, that belief in God must undermine intellectual pursuits and especially the pursuit of scientific knowledge. You may already know, for example, that Richard Dawkins wrote articles crowning his fellow atheists as "brights," strongly implying that believers are less intelligent than they are.[20] And you may agree with him. Yet among the ranks of believers are not just intelligent people but authentic geniuses from all over the world. They're philosophers, artists, statesmen and, yes, scientists who've laid the foundation for civilization and taken the laboring oar for progress for thousands of years, men like Socrates, William of Ockam, Erasmus, Rembrandt, Bach, Newton and Lincoln. Acknowledge the fact that they were brilliant thinkers *and* believers and it'll disabuse you of the notion that faith and reason are incompatible. Make the existence of God your hypothesis. You don't have to believe it; just test it. It'll be enough to open your mind to follow the evidence wherever it leads.

---

20. Dawkins, "The Future Looks Bright."

I

Him

What's in a Name?

God said to Moses, "I am who I am." And he said, "Say this to the people of Israel: 'I am has sent me to you.'"

Before we begin, we should be clear about the God whose existence is our hypothesis. He is the God of the Bible; we'll learn about him through the old and new testaments.

When we want to get to know someone we usually start with his name, and tucked away in the Old Testament is a dramatic story about what God calls himself. Moses was tending a flock in the wilderness, quietly minding his business, when he saw something strange and otherworldly; it was an angel "in flames of fire" within a bush that didn't burn (Exod 3:2 NIV). He was witnessing a miracle. When he started walking toward it, he heard God tell him to stop in his tracks. "Do not come any closer," God warned him (Exod 3:5 NIV). He told Moses to remove his sandals because the ground on which he stood wasn't what it appeared to be. "The place where you are standing," God said, "is holy ground" (Exod 3:5 NIV).

The encounter staggered Moses. He was overwhelmed and hid his face in fear, but God wasn't through with him yet. Now he gave him a mission; he told Moses to go to Pharaoh and liberate the Israelites from their Egyptian oppressors. And when Moses doubted his ability to accomplish his will, God told him that he and the people of Israel wouldn't be alone in their quest. He promised Moses, "I will be with you" (Exod 3:12 NIV).

When it was all over, Moses gathered himself. But before he assembled the elders to let them know what God wanted them to do, he asked God a question. "Suppose I go to the Israelites and say to them, 'The God of your fathers has sent me to you,' and they ask me, 'What is his name?' Then what shall I tell them?" (Exod 3:13 NIV)

Moses probably thought it was a simple question. When God answered him, however, his answer wasn't what Moses expected, or what anyone would expect.

He called himself "I Am" (Exod 3:14 NIV).

It was a strange response but the circumstances explain why God responded the way he did. He called himself "I Am" because the God who could perform miracles, and who would eventually free a captive people from a powerful monarch so they could conquer a Promised Land, was not a God who'd have a common name.

A common name usually links its subject with something else; your last name means you're part of a family of course, but names also tie people to familiar things like places (there are Underhills and Hightowers, Brooks and Rivers, Londons and Yorks); trades (we've all met Smiths, Taylors and Weavers); or a particular characteristic (Faith, Hope or Charity to pick a few . . .). Eventually Moses' people would come to know the Assyrians. Their god was named Ashur, which linked him to Assur, the capital of their mighty empire. And from that point forward their god was as vital as their kingdom—which has since vanished.

God's message for Moses was that he wasn't the offspring of someone else; he couldn't be characterized by a mere virtue or trait; he shouldn't be associated with a single place or empire. He was greater than any of these things. The miracle that Moses witnessed, and the mission that he gave him, should have made that clear.

"I Am" didn't leave Moses empty-handed, however. Unlike a common name, "I Am" communicated something much more important—insights into his powerful and mysterious nature.

He told Moses that he was one; he said *I* am.

He told Moses that he exists for eternity. He said he was the God of "your fathers" and will be the God of his people "from generation to generation" (Exod 3:15 NIV). I Am, he said, "is my name forever" (Exod 3:15 NIV).

And he showed Moses that he was a spiritual being; his angel was engulfed in flames without burning the bush around it. He existed outside of physical space.

All of these attributes flow naturally from the commonplace definition of God as the perfect, supreme and infinite being. If he is perfect then he has no superior, and if he is supreme, he has no equal; therefore he must be one. And if he is infinite then he can't be contained and measured in physical space, meaning he's spiritual; and time cannot age him, meaning he's eternal.

These descriptions of God's nature shouldn't be controversial to anyone. Whether or not you believe in him, the God of the Bible has always been described as such.

There is a problem, however. Words like infinite, perfect and supreme really don't define him or bring him that much closer to us; they're just generalities that make God seem more remote than present. When we speak of him in these terms we sound like a school girl describing her first crush. God's just so . . . dreamy.

It's a problem for anyone who thinks about God, even the most sophisticated professors and philosophers. They traffic in generalities, too; they just substitute clinical terms like "omniscient," "omnipotent" and "omnipresent" for dreamy. It sounds smarter; the academic journals demand it.

If we want to get closer to God, labeling him or spinning theories about him will only get us so far. Filling our minds with generalities is like filling a balloon with air; we become intellectual lightweights, "puffed up" with words that signify very little. To paraphrase G.K. Chesterton, the humble believer only wants to get his head into the heavens but the egotistical theologian tries to get the heavens into his head. And like a balloon, it is his head that pops.[1]

We should know better. Geniuses as diverse as Aquinas and Einstein have recognized the limits of the human mind. If they were right that we can't comprehend the cosmos or even exhaust the essence of a fly, then we certainly can't comprehend their Creator.

A work of art usually says something about the artist. Since reality is complex, doesn't it make sense that its Creator would be too? If we want to get to know God, we shouldn't slap a label on him. Instead, we should draw closer to him, see him at work in the world and experience his presence. We won't fully understand him, but we will learn about him.

And what we learn may surprise us. Contrary to what many believers expect and the common claim of atheists that he's just the protagonist in a fairytale, our encounter with him won't always be pleasant.

The hymn *Nearer My God To Thee* tells us so. It isn't about how we define or think about God; it's about how we experience his presence. And the experience more often than not is difficult for us. The hymn is solemn and slow, lamenting the "cross that raiseth me," and that "darkness be over me, my rest a stone." Ultimately the hymn's author says it is "by my woes" that he is brought "nearer my God to Thee."

It's a tough message. We prefer to think that God is love (and for Christians and many others, he is), but we should beware of that generality too; it can mislead us into thinking that our relationship with him is all about ease and comfort and feelings of affection and contentedness. The hymn says otherwise; our relationship with God, just like our relationships with the people we love, is more complicated than it appears at first; it has a disturbing side that can include fears and anxieties, and even pains and burdens.

---

1. Chesterton wrote, "The poet only asks to get his head into the heavens. It is the logician who seeks to get the heavens into his head. And it is his head that splits." Chesterton, *Orthodoxy*, 29.

Nearer My God To Thee is based on a story in Genesis. It's about Jacob and the two different ways in which he encounters God. First, he rests his head on a stone and meets God in a dream in which God promises him power and prosperity. Jacob sees "a stairway resting on the earth, with its top reaching to heaven.... There above it stood the Lord" (Gen 28:12-13 NIV). Then God makes Jacob a promise in words that are simple and clear:

> I will give you and your descendants the land on which you are lying. Your descendants will be like the dust of the earth, and you will spread out to the west and to the east, to the north and to the south. All peoples on earth will be blessed through you and your offspring. I am with you and will watch over you wherever you go, and I will bring you back to this land. I will not leave you until I have done what I have promised you (Gen 28:13-15 NIV).

Jacob wakes up inspired, ready for his mission. The land on which he is lying, he says, is "awesome"; it is "the house of God" and "the gate of heaven" (Gen 28:17 NIV). He's going to do God's will and bless the world with his descendants in the land that God has promised him, the very house of God. His path is clear ...

... until things get complicated. He meets his uncle Laban and falls in love with his beautiful daughter Rachel. Laban promises Rachel's hand in marriage in exchange for Jacob's labor. Jacob agrees to the deal but in the dark of night Laban slips his older and less attractive daughter, Leah, into Jacob's tent. When the sun comes up, Jacob's a little miffed. Laban knows how much Jacob wants Rachel so he extracts more labor from Jacob in exchange for her.

Now Rachel and Leah are jealous for Jacob's love and attention. They each try to produce more children than the other and Jacob consents to let them try; it's God's will, after all, that his descendants scatter north, south, east and west, which as far as Jacob is concerned means that he has a divine sanction to use them to sire a nation.

While Jacob spends his nights doing God's will, he spends his days plotting to make Laban's herds of sheep and goats his own. And when Laban takes a trip he does just that, which angers

Laban. Jacob bolts with Laban's daughters and the herds of animals that don't belong to him. Laban gives chase and they finally meet and make an uneasy peace, just in time for Jacob to find out that his brother, Esau, is coming after him with an army.

These were turbulent times for this mercurial man.

Now Jacob encounters God for a second time. This time God doesn't appear in a dream; he appears as a man, flesh and blood. He isn't situated at the top of a stairway leading to Heaven; he meets Jacob in his tent. He doesn't give Jacob any commands; Jacob wrestles with him. And when God found that he couldn't overpower Jacob on a human level, he summoned his power and, as the Bible puts it, he simply "touched" Jacob's hip so that it "was wrenched" (Gen 32:25 NIV). Then God, still in the form of a man, spoke to Jacob:

> "Let me go, for it is daybreak."
>
> But Jacob replied, "I will not let you go unless you bless me."
>
> The man asked him, "What is your name?"
>
> "Jacob," he answered.
>
> Then the man said, "Your name will no longer be Jacob, but Israel, because you have struggled with God and with humans and have overcome."
>
> Jacob said, "Please tell me your name."
>
> But he replied, "Why do you ask my name?" Then he blessed him there.
>
> So Jacob called the place Peniel, saying, "It is because I saw God face to face, and yet my life was spared." (Gen 32:26–30 NIV)

God was no longer a figure in Jacob's dreams. Their relationship changed when Jacob met him up close; it became difficult and complex. They struggled, not quite seeing eye to eye, but not as bitter and irreconcilable adversaries; it was a struggle between a servant and his master in which the servant refused to let go until he got his master's blessing and help.

Jacob was an unsavory character in many ways but his redeeming quality was his desire to follow and have a relationship with God. He wrestled with him, in part because he wrestled with everyone but mostly because he wanted his blessing. So the master relented and, as Martin Luther is supposed to have said, God went on to "draw a straight line with a crooked stick." And Israel was born.

Notice that when Jacob encountered God he, too, asked for his name, just like Moses would after him. This time it seems like a reasonable question. Jacob knew how powerful he was; God's touch by itself almost crippled him. This ambitious and proud man who worked and schemed to get what he wanted, had to admit to himself that he needed God to fulfill his dream; he knew he couldn't succeed alone. He wanted to know his name because he thought of God as a companion.

We can credit Moses with the same desire. When he asked God for his name, the question wasn't impertinent; instead it was born of his desire for a relationship between God and his people. Like Jacob before him, he wanted to know God's name not to limit him, but to call upon him.

When we're told that God is omnipresent, omniscient and omnipotent, we're told very little about him that we can grasp. The story of Jacob, on the other hand, is the story about God living and breathing in his relationship with man. And it was a close relationship. God was present in a tent, of all places, in the middle of a desert; he knew what nobody else could have imagined, that a "crooked stick" like Jacob would become the patriarch of a nation of his chosen people; and he showed his power by disabling Jacob with a "touch," merely checking his wayward disposition when he could have broken this crooked stick of a man. God's presence, knowledge and power are part of the story, but his relationship with Jacob *is* the story.

Jacob's life was by turns a comedy and a drama and always colorful and meaningful. In his relationship with God we get a glimpse of his nature and purposes which, if not fully revealed, are illuminated to an extent that we know him better. It's the story of a man to whom a living God appeared. There are many such stories in the Bible and elsewhere, a wonderful variety of encounters from which we can learn who he is.

We accept a hypothesis as true when it's supported by reality and by what we know and experience in the world around us. In order to test our hypothesis then, we should take our cue from the story of Jacob and look for him, not only above us and in our dreams, but everywhere and all around us. After all if God exists and is omnipresent (to make some use of that generality) he deserves no less. Paul wrote that God's "invisible qualities—his eternal power and divine nature—have been clearly seen, being understood from what has been made . . ." (Rom 1:20 NIV). So let's examine some of the curious facts from human history and our daily lives and see if God is behind them, helping to explain, as he did to Jacob, the depth of our struggles and the richness of our blessings.

II

Science

*The Shadows
of a God*

"What is this quintessence of dust?"—Hamlet

"What can be more curious," Charles Darwin thought, "than that the hand of a man, formed for grasping, that of a mole for digging, the leg of the horse, the paddle of the porpoise, and the wing of the bat, should all be constructed on the same pattern, and should include the same bones, in the same relative positions?"[1]

Darwin's observations launched over a century of scientific research into how different species evolved from their ancestors, and the work continues today. Scientists now believe that life on earth began as a single cell and evolved into modern man. The whole process took about four billion years, give or take, and innumerable mutations produced millions of species. If you're inclined to study such things then the evolution of life must be fascinating in all of its variety and complexity.

What can be more curious? For one thing, even though the first chapter in the Bible's Book of Genesis says that God created

---

1. Darwin, *Origin of the Species*, 472.

everything in six days, it's remarkably consistent with Darwin's theory of evolution.

That's because the author of Genesis wanted us to read his story of creation figuratively; we can't read it literally because it contains glaring contradictions. For example, in chapter one, it says that God separated the light from the darkness in fundamentally different ways. On the first day of creation, God "separated the light from the darkness" (Gen 1:4 NIV) simply by saying "Let there be light" (Gen 1:3 NIV), which was a miracle; but on the fourth day of creation, God created the sun and the moon "to separate light from darkness" through a natural process (Gen 1:18 NIV).

There's a similar contradiction between chapters one and two. Chapter two says that vegetation was supposed to grow naturally; it says that there was no vegetation because there wasn't any "rain on the earth and there was no one to work the ground" (Gen 2:5 NIV). However, chapter one says that God created vegetation miraculously; it says that on the third day of creation, before there was anyone to work the ground, God said "'let the land produce vegetation' . . . and it was so" (Gen 1:11 NIV).

Why would God make the same thing twice, and how could he make it through both a miracle and a natural process? It's the type of question atheists ask all the time, if only to mock the ignorance of those believers who also read chapter one literally, putting their faith at odds with their reason. They're easy prey for atheists who would rather provoke an argument over the story's details than join a conversation about the story's meaning.

And the most frequent source of mockery is in the first chapter of Genesis, where it says that God made everything in six days. If you read the story like an atheist, you seize on the fact that it's at odds with science and simply incredible. You read the story literally and mock what it says. You know that all of those animals, vegetables and minerals couldn't have come into being in such a short period of time; you know that it's ridiculous to claim that they did; and you think that any book whose opening chapter is so blatantly ignorant is probably best shelved. Nothing about it excites your curiosity.

SCIENCE

But if you read the story like a believer, it does excite your curiosity. You keep reading, not because you think it's literally true, but for another reason; you're struck by the fact that God seems to have worked, not incredibly quickly, but surprisingly slowly. Precisely because you believe in him, you know that he's capable of performing miracles and creating things spontaneously; he could have willed everything into existence in an instant. Yet in God's original act of creation he spends six full days at work, making everything carefully and deliberately. He's like an Olympic athlete who takes five minutes to run a mile; five minutes isn't a long time, unless you know who's running the race. And so unlike the atheist, you read the story and wonder why it took him so long to finish what he started; you probe beneath the details for the story's meaning. And when you do, it leads you to a startling conclusion—that the message in the first chapter of Genesis is not that God created everything quickly (and in a time frame that science contradicts); rather, it's that he created everything in a way that, for God at least, was unusually slow, incremental and progressive, as if he was working through a rational process.

And your faith may lead you to notice something else, too—that the order of creation in chapter one is actually consistent with the theory of evolution. It says that God made all living things progressively, starting with the lower organisms and ending with the higher forms of life. After creating light and darkness, the sky and the world, the land and the sea, God made vegetation and then fish, fowl and beasts. And then, finally, man. As G. K. Chesterton wrote,

> If evolution simply means that a positive thing called an ape turned very slowly into a positive thing called a man, then it is stingless for the most orthodox; for a personal God might just as well do things slowly as quickly, especially if, like the Christian God, he were outside time.[2]

If believers reject the theory of evolution and atheists reject the story of creation because they think they're incompatible, they

---

2. Chesterton, *Orthodoxy*, 60–61.

should consider the possibility that the author of Genesis might have disagreed.

Believers should remember that God can make something through the laws of nature that he decreed, just as well as he can make something through a miracle. We can accept, without denying our faith, that God can form man through a biological process that culminates in man sharing the likeness of his Creator. In short, just because we understand the science of biology (or some of it), doesn't mean God has nothing to do with it. The believer "is quite free to believe," Chesterton wrote, "that there is a considerable amount of settled order and inevitable development in the universe."[3]

Nonetheless, Chesterton wrote, it's not all settled order and inevitable development; the believer also "admits that the universe is manifold and even miscellaneous."[4] And so if God wanted to emphasize that he created us in his image and that we're "fearfully and wonderfully made," it would also make sense that he would do it through four billion years of work that would leave us all awestruck (Ps 139:14 NIV). Those who study evolution should especially feel that sense of awe; they know better than anyone that, while we may understand some of it, the formation of man is ultimately incomprehensible. Science, too, can make us wonder at his ways. The more we learn about how he works, the more it fills us with wonder about him and makes us marvel at his creation. Like Kepler and Einstein said, we understand parts of creation and wonder at its creator.

It's a lesson for believers and atheists alike. God works through miracles but there's no reason to think that he works *only* through miracles. The Lord works in mysterious—and rational—ways. We understand some of the rational ways in which he works. At the same time, because we know we'll never comprehend it all, we can be dazzled by his rational processes and his inexplicable miracles.

---

3. Chesterton, *Orthodoxy*, 41.
4. Chesterton, *Orthodoxy*, 42.

SCIENCE

Every living thing continues to evolve and adapt, and man's no exception. Believers who worship a living God should welcome this insight too; a living God is always present and involved in our lives, including our physical development. Of course not everything that happens in the natural world or to the human body is his doing, just as the state of our soul isn't always his doing (there are other forces at work . . .); but it would be foolish to suppose that he plays no role at all in our continuing physical development. At no point did his physical creation of man come to a grinding halt.

Atheists and believers who read the story of creation literally are the opposite sides of the same counterfeit coin; they both think faith and reason are irreconcilable. The atheist sacrifices his faith for his reason; the believer sacrifices his reason for his faith. The truth, however, is that the theory of evolution, as an explanation for the physical development of man, simply expresses scientifically what the Bible says in a story.

* * *

There's another contradiction in the story of creation, except this one isn't about its details. It involves two major themes so we need to focus on it.

In the first two chapters of Genesis, the whole order of creation runs in opposite directions. Chapter one, as we noted, says that God made all living things progressively, starting with the lower organisms and ending with the higher forms of life, culminating in man. But in chapter two, God created man first and then, seeing that he was lonely, he said that he "will make a helper suitable for him" (Gen 2:18 NIV). So he formed the animals *after* he made man and then, when "no suitable helper was found," he created woman (Gen 2:20 NIV).[5]

---

5. It's true that some translations say that God "had formed" the animals, suggesting that he'd created them sometime before man. But the overwhelming majority of translations say that he created man before the animals because that's what the story's context clearly indicates; God said that he "will make" a helper for man and the very next verse mentions the creation of the animals (and to take the point a little further, "had formed" is a verb in the pluperfect

We have to acknowledge such a stark and fundamental inconsistency. It's too obvious to casually dismiss as a thoughtless oversight by a sloppy writer, which leaves us with an interesting possibility—that the author intentionally included it in his story because it's critical to its meaning.

And in fact it is. The opposing orders of creation illuminate the unique nature and history of man; they reflect the tension at the core of his being.

To see how this is so, let's get right to the meaning of the story of creation. The fundamental message in the story is that God created man and gave him a dual mandate of sorts. He gave man the right to rule over his creation (so the first chapter is about God creating man in his image and giving him dominion over the earth), but also the duty to rule according to his will (and so the second chapter is about God creating Adam and Eve, who receive his commands and are supposed to be his servants).

The first two chapters detail this mandate to rule and to serve, and the tension that it creates in human nature. The first chapter of Genesis presents man as the crowning achievement of a gradual process of physical creation. As we mentioned earlier, God creates life progressively; he begins with plants and trees, works his way up the food chain and finishes by empowering his ultimate creation, which is man. God creates man in his image and he makes more than one of him (hence, "mankind"); he forms "mankind in his own image, in the image of God he created them, male and female he created them" (Gen 1:27 NIV). He also blesses them; he tells them to be fruitful and multiply, and he gives them dominion over the earth so they can subdue it. And while he says the rest of creation is "good," God declares his creation of mankind "very good" (Gen 1:31 NIV).

In chapter one, human beings are powerful and dominant physical creations. They're the viceroys of God.

In chapter two, creation takes a pivotal turn; man becomes a spiritual being. The scene is much different than it was in chapter

---

tense, but the original Hebrew doesn't have a pluperfect tense; the Hebrew word used in this passage is, simply, "formed.").

SCIENCE

one where God, in a prodigious display of his power, made the whole world any every living thing. In chapter two things settle down (or seem to at first . . .). All we see is a small garden, a solitary human being, two mysterious trees and a snake (one that talks, again giving fodder to the atheist who reads the story literally). The rest of creation—all of the fish, fowl and animals—either move off stage or are bit players that God dismisses because they're not suitable helpers for man.

Man's the focus but his connection to the earth is barely acknowledged and hardly celebrated; it says in passing that God formed man from the "dust of the ground," downplaying his physical constitution and making you wonder what's so special about him (Gen 2:7 NIV). But then God did something else; in contrast to chapter one's patient, verse by verse, physical creation of life over six days, in one verse in chapter two God suddenly breathed "the breath of life" into man and man "became a living being" (Gen 2:7 NIV).

The contrast between the two chapters is striking and appears deliberate, as if the author was pointing out and what distinguishes man from every other living thing.

In the original Hebrew the words for breath—*nᵉšāmâ* in chapter two of Genesis, and *rûaḥ* elsewhere—are synonymous with spirit. So when God breathed his spirit into man, man was no longer just a physical being made in his likeness or image; he became a spiritual being too.

He had the breath of God within him and shared some of God's characteristics. One of them was the ability to love; Eve came into being because, God said, "It is not good for the man to be alone" (Gen 2:18 NIV). This was when human love was born.

If that makes you think that becoming a spiritual being is a playful fairytale, the author of the second chapter of Genesis thought differently. The story of creation tells us that Adam and Eve shared another of God's characteristics, one that proved difficult for them to bear; it was the ability to choose, including the choice to obey or disobey their Creator. The snake was the catalyst for this especially consequential choice that they would make. And when the time came for Adam and Eve to make that choice, they kicked up quite a storm. Just one chapter tells the story of man disobeying God and choosing instead to rely on his own knowledge and power; of God expelling him from Eden; and of man facing death with the memory of eternity in Eden still fresh in his mind. This was when human sin was born.

It all happened so rapidly; in an instant the knowledge of good and evil, and of time and eternity, became part of man's nature. The poet William Blake expressed it well; in man, he wrote,

> Joy and woe are woven fine,
> a clothing for the soul divine.[6]

In short, what came out of Eden was modern man. When he emerged there was no other creature like him.

And he also bore a unique burden. He struggled in a way that's entirely different from all other creatures, who merely struggled to survive. Man's nature included incompatible elements—evil and good, and death and eternity—so he struggled with the world *and* himself.

Suddenly mere survival wasn't enough for him; exercising dominion over the earth and subduing everything on it didn't banish the evil within him or satisfy his longing for eternity. Man had a problem to solve. From then on he wasn't merely a creature of the earth who wanted to survive; he was a creator who was conscious of eternity. He didn't just build huts for shelter; he built pyramids for the dead.

The world had never seen anything like him. He felt the struggle between good and evil within and around him, and his creations showed it; he felt confined by time and death, but he also felt liberated by the breath of life and eternity, so he strove to create something permanent. Billions of years in the making, man's story got very interesting, very quickly.

The change was instantaneous and dramatic. While the evolution of life began four billion years ago and man's closest relatives, the primates, evolved over millions of years, it was just a few

---

6. Blake, *Auguries of Innocence*, lines 59–60.

thousand years ago—a blink of the evolutionary eye—when man began to make his mark. Suddenly:

Man was an engineer and a lawmaker. The Egyptians built the Pyramids at Giza; the whole complex is a marvel and scholars still don't understand how they did it. And Moses wrote the Pentateuch for his people; it includes the Ten Commandments that laid the foundation for thousands of years of religious beliefs and ethical standards.

The Greeks built the Parthenon and gave the world the Iliad and the Odyssey, Homer's epic poems in dactylic hexameter that became the template for heroic tales and storytelling. Centuries later in Athens, the Golden Age of Greek civilization passed as the philosopher Socrates drank hemlock rather than betray his ethical principles. And a few centuries after that, Alexander the Great supposedly wept because "I am not yet the lord of one world"[7] and proceeded to spread Greek civilization through a series of bloody conquests; he established an empire and died at age thirty-three.

The Romans founded a republic and built an intricate network of roads; they left a legacy in engineering and law that revealed their practical genius, and their zeal for war and relentless pursuit of their enemies laid the foundation for their empire. Their appetite for power stung all sorts of people; among the roads that the Romans built was the Appian Way, where Crassus crucified 6000 slaves because they and their leader, Spartacus, rebelled against their masters. Yet there were other motives for rebellion and more subtle ways to rebel; the disciple Peter was a solitary martyr who confounded the authorities by choosing crucifixion over betraying his belief in his Savior.

In the sixth century the religion of Islam emerged from the deserts of the Middle East. It unified warring tribes through the faith that "there is no God but Allah, and Mohammed is His prophet." When Mohammed's successors sent their armies with that message into the heart of modern France in 732, Charles Martel stopped them at the Battle of Tours. In the ninth

---

7. The statement is probably apocryphal but we know enough about Alexander to assert that, if he didn't say it, he should have.

century Martel's grandson, Charlemagne, founded the Holy Roman Empire by forcibly uniting parts of Europe under the Catholic Church; he and his successors would fight to reconquer the rest of Europe from the Muslims and lead crusades into the Middle East for centuries. Ultimately unity was hard to achieve, as both the Muslim and Christian faiths divided into sects that warred among themselves.

In 1215 the Archbishop of Canterbury drafted Magna Carta, which diminished the power of England's King John and his successors; the king was forced to acknowledge that

> ... the Church of England shall be free.... We have also granted to all the freemen of this kingdom, for us and our heirs forever, all the underwritten liberties...[8]

Now the monarch's will wasn't always law and in many ways the monarch himself became subject to the law.

The matter wasn't permanently and universally settled however. In the sixteenth century, King Henry VIII claimed that the king was the supreme head of the church (and beheaded Thomas More for refusing to swear an oath acknowledging it). In the late eighteenth century, Thomas Jefferson wrote the Declaration of Independence and claimed that King George III abused his power by violating the rights with which all men were "endowed by their Creator" (and he risked being drawn and quartered for it); in the early nineteenth century he wrote a letter to the Danbury Baptist Association trumpeting "the wall of separation between Church and State" (and risked the political support of churches that were funded by the state). And in the twentieth century, communists Vladimir Lenin and Joseph Stalin claimed that the state had the right to abolish the church (and they executed over 100,000 clergymen to make their point).

Man worked and accumulated wealth in increasingly sophisticated economies. At first he bartered goods; the Lydians coined money around 700 BC; and in 1792, twenty-four stockbrokers met under a buttonwood tree on Wall Street and created

---

8. McKechnie, *Magna Carta*, 222.

the New York Stock Exchange, where Warren Buffet and Bernie Madoff made fortunes.

He was an artist, too.

He could be a sculptor. The City of Florence commissioned Michelangelo for a work to adorn its cathedral; he spent four years sculpting King David in marble. Four centuries later, Adolph Hitler made Arno Breker the official sculptor for the third reich; he spent a decade cranking out dozens of sculptures and portraits that glorified German fascism, individual Nazis and their sympathizers around the world.

He could be a filmmaker. He made films from *A Man For All Seasons*, to *My Fair Lady*, to *Silence of the Lambs*, all of them winning Oscars for Best Picture.

He could also write poems, plays and novels; dance, sing and compose; paint canvas and take pictures. What he made reflected who he was in so many ways.

And he made war. In 1945 he firebombed Dresden for three days and leveled Hiroshima in a few seconds. It echoed what had happened thousands of years earlier when Cato the Elder demanded the destruction of Carthage—*Carthago delenda est!*—and Roman legions complied, decimating Hannibal's birthplace and salting its fields so the vanquished could never return.

Darwin wondered what could be more curious than the similarities between a man's hand and a bat's wing. The answer is, a lot.

And it all happened very recently. Before man came on the scene, a four billion year slog through innumerable mutations didn't produce a single species that changed the world. But after billions of years of evolution man suddenly became a creator and destroyer, changing the world unlike all of the other life forms that were mere creatures of it.

What explains this recent, sudden and radical departure from billions of years of evolution?

Our hypothesis is, chapter two of Genesis and the breath of God, which gave man a soul and suddenly motivated him to transcend his existence. That's why he could change the world in a few thousand years after a billion years of physical evolution had failed to produce a species that could do anything of the sort. The gift of God's spirit manifested itself in the dawning of history.

Atheists are right that the origin of man stretches back billions of years; the theory of evolution goes a long way toward explaining his physical constitution. Believers are right that the creation of man occurred only a few thousand years ago, if by that they mean that's when God made man a spiritual creature. But it's the Bible's revelation that God breathed the breath of life into man that's most important. It's indispensable to understanding human history, not to mention human nature; and it explains why, just a few thousand years ago, man suddenly changed the world.

The first chapter of Genesis is the story of man's physical creation, which is consistent with science; and the second chapter is the story of man's spiritual creation, which is consistent with history. In the first chapter, God makes man in his image, and man is a proud ruler; and in the second chapter, God gives him free will, and man is a fallen servant. Taken as a whole, they suggest that man is a uniquely complex and, yes, contradictory creature—just as the contradictions in the order of creation suggest.[9]

* * *

---

9. Whether we should read the Bible figuratively is, of course, an important issue, one that especially concerns its narrative passages (almost everyone agrees that the Bible's poetry, for example, should be read figuratively). Many believers worry that reading one narrative figuratively gives us a license to read them all that way so that, eventually, we'll stumble into serious errors; for example, if we read the Bible's historical passages figuratively we may find ourselves believing that the Israelite's exodus and Jesus' crucifixion never really happened.

But there's no reason to worry; the text itself tells us how we should read it. Historical narratives present facts that must be read literally; narratives in the form of parables and allegories use metaphors that must be read figuratively. The Bible contains both forms of text (and many others). We must read them as the authors intended them to be read, consistent with the form of text that the authors chose, not arbitrarily or because we want to make the Bible conform to our own beliefs; in this way our decision about when to read the Bible figuratively is firmly grounded in the text itself.

SCIENCE

In 1831 Alexis DeTocqueville left France to study American politics, culture and religion. His book *Democracy in America* is so insightful that it reads less like an analysis and more like a biography of the United States; he gets that close to the essence of how Americans think and act. Along the way he takes a lot of thoughtful detours in which he offers his own opinions on a variety of topics. One such detour is especially interesting.

In a chapter about religion in America, he wrote about man's dissatisfaction with the world and desire for a better place in which to thrive. His observations were a nineteenth century version of the modern epigram about man being *in* the world but not *of* it. He showed how man's sense of good and evil, and his consciousness of death and eternity, led him to strive for God:

> The short space of threescore years can never content the imagination of man; nor can the imperfect joys of this world satisfy his heart. Man alone, of all created beings, displays a natural contempt of existence, and yet a boundless desire to exist; he scorns life, but he dreads annihilation. These different feelings incessantly urged his soul to the contemplation of a future state, and religion directs his musings there. Religion, then, is simply another form of hope; and it is no less natural to the human heart than hope itself. Men cannot abandon their religious faith without a kind of aberration of intellect, and a sort of violent distortion of their true natures.[10]

Unlike the rest of creation, man's got religion. The word itself signifies the striving that characterizes us. It's derived from the Latin *ligare*, which means to bind. Through religion we seek to re-bind ourselves to God.

And that brings us back to Darwin, whose theory does exactly the opposite; it binds man to the earth. Darwin tells us that, fundamentally, man evolves, and that's all; we are animals and we want to survive, and nothing more. The difference between man and the higher animals, "great as it is," says Darwin, "certainly is one

---

10. de Tocqueville, *Democracy*, 359.

of degree and not of kind."[11] He even went so far as to say that "there is no fundamental difference between man and the higher mammals in their mental faculties."[12]

Darwin goes on to say that at the bottom of everything we do, there's only a struggle to survive. He wrote that, like all life on earth, we follow "one general law," namely, "let the strongest live and the weakest die."[13] This is "natural selection" or the "struggle for existence," although he eventually conceded that Herbert Spencer's grim "Survival of the Fittest is more accurate."[14]

It's a poor description of man and it's no explanation at all for why man changed the world.

We can see this most clearly in Darwin's belief that man's struggle to survive is the foundation for his morals and ethics. It's the best example of how the theory of evolution falls flat as an explanation of human nature.

His theory sounds promising enough at first. He thought the struggle to survive produced "social instincts [that] afforded the basis for the development of the moral sense."[15] Basically, man learned that he was more likely to survive in a strong and cohesive society than if he lived alone, so he slowly developed social instincts and rules of behavior that encouraged cooperation, which is how man's regard for other people increased over time. According to Darwin, this is how we became moral creatures; the instinct to survive evolved into morality.

Here's how Darwin broke it down: When man acted "for the good of others," he claimed, he won the approval of the people around him and society as a whole, which "undoubtedly is the highest pleasure on this earth"; which made his "higher impulses" into something "habitual" that "may almost be called instincts"; which "by degrees" made it "intolerable for him to obey his sensuous passions"; so, therefore, the "rule of life" for man was simply

---

11. Darwin, *Descent of Man*, 105.
12. Darwin, *Descent of Man*, 35.
13. Darwin, *Origin of the Species*, 244.
14. Darwin, *Origin of the Species*, 72.
15. Darwin, *Descent of Man*, 404.

to follow what he thinks are his strongest and best "impulses and instincts."[16] And thus man's struggle to survive produced instincts and habits that, guided by his advanced intelligence, "naturally lead to the golden rule."[17]

Ever since Darwin made these claims, anthropologists and biologists have expanded on them, marshalling reams of detail to support his fundamentally simple thesis. Oliver Scott Curry is one of them. He's the director of the Oxford Morals Project at University of Oxford's Institute of Cognitive and Evolutionary Anthropology. "Morality," he wrote, "is a collection of tools for promoting cooperation."[18] He even went so far as to say that cooperation "is always and everywhere considered moral."[19]

It's all very simple, too simple in fact, and this is where things start to fall apart. Darwin's attempt to connect evolution and morals is contrived and tenuous, and Curry's reduction of morals to tools of cooperation is clever but facile.[20] The consequences of their arguments make this clear.

Basing morality on cooperating with your fellow man and winning his approval sounds innocent enough but when you scroll through history and common experience, it can be dangerous. Man has done so much evil with the approval and cooperation of others. On a personal scale Bonnie and Clyde were allies, and

---

16. Barlow, *The Autobiography of Charles Darwin*, 94.
17. Darwin, *Descent of Man*, 106.
18. Curry, "Morality as Cooperation," 28.
19. Curry, Mullins and Whitehouse, "Is It Good To Cooperate," 59.
20. And Darwin's explanation of morals is especially noxious for believers, undermining our faith in God in a very insidious way. Darwin doesn't honestly and explicitly deny God's existence; he just makes him irrelevant by claiming that man doesn't "need" God to get along with his fellow creatures. Regardless of whether God exists, Darwin wrote, "man can do his duty" (Darwin, *Charles Darwin: His Life*, 57). Those "tools for promoting cooperation" are sufficient for man's purposes because they satisfy his instinct to survive. God's existence therefore isn't an urgent issue for us; we can rest assured, he wrote dismissively, that it "is beyond the scope of man's intellect" (Darwin, *Charles Darwin: His Life*, 57). Likewise whether man has an immortal soul is something "every man must judge for himself between conflicting vague probabilities" (Darwin, *Charles Darwin: His Life*, 57).

gangs, cartels and mafia families run cooperative "enterprises." Social circles can include lovers like Eva Braun (Hitler's mistress) and sycophants like Joseph Goebbels (Hitler's minister of propaganda). In society as a whole, masses of people throughout history and into the present day have formed cults of personality; the rapturous and ecstatic devotion to Hitler, successive North Korean dictators and Iranian ayatollahs comes to mind.

This is why so many brutal societies have overpowered their more civilized contemporaries; they too can be characterized by strength and cooperation. Militant Sparta defeated democratic Athens in the Peloponnesian War; republican Rome granted some liberties to its plebs but increasingly indulged its appetite for conquest and slavery, laying the foundation for its successor, imperial Rome (from the republic of Cicero to the empire of bread and circuses . . . *there's* the descent of man).

And mankind's uneven record as a moral and just being has not only continued unabated into modern times, arguably it has worsened. Had Darwin foreseen that man in the twentieth century would cooperate in forming authoritarian, fascist and communist societies out of cultures that were already strong and cohesive, but that would nonetheless become responsible for two world wars and the genocides of tens of millions, he might have been less enthusiastic about how man behaves when he follows his impulses and instincts for the approval of others.

In fact the most brutal societies in history have seduced their followers with a promise of peace, order and security, appealing to the very instinct for survival that Darwin celebrated as the foundation of morality. Think of what it means to be a part of a "thousand year reich," communist empire or Islamic caliphate that spans the globe. And by appealing to other instincts that are just as strong and likely to win the approval of society as the instinct to survive (like the exercise of power and the thrill of conquering anyone who opposes your race, ideology or religion), they've lead their followers to fight and kill for it.

They all believed that they were engaged in a struggle for existence, one that would usher in an age of cooperation and harmony, profoundly enhancing man's prospects for survival.

They believed that they were the fittest to survive.

Let the strongest live and the weakest die.

Our recent history shows that "tools of cooperation" only accomplish so much. They're like the rules of the road; they may help you survive by reducing traffic accidents but they don't tell you where you're supposed to go. Man's most revered moral codes, from the Ten Commandments to the Sermon on the Mount, do tell you where you should and shouldn't go (often contrary to your own interests, and sometimes at the risk of your own welfare and even your life).[21]

And they're not negotiable; there's no commandment that forbids you to lie and Jesus didn't preach that you should love your enemy, "*unless...*". Darwin's code of cooperation, however, is like a contract that comes with conditions, limitations and fine print that the parties can negotiate: I will be my brother's keeper, *provided* my brother fulfills his duty to me and enhances my prospects for survival; I am a patriot, *however*, I won't ask what I can do for my country *until* my country shows what it can do for me.

* * *

21. Curry, Mullins and Whitehouse list seven types of cooperation in an attempt to show how their theory can serve as a moral compass. They claim that the cooperative behaviors that are "always and everywhere good" are: loyalty to family; loyalty to group; reciprocity; exercising power; obeying authority; dividing resources according to bargaining power and notions of fairness; and property rights. There are two defects in their theory, however: First, none of these behaviors account for selfless acts of love, where the welfare of someone else is all that matters. Second, these behaviors often conflict, as when bargaining power and notions of fairness lead to different outcomes, or when your loyalty to your family conflicts with your loyalty to your neighbor. In these instances Curry, Mullins and Whitehouse say their theory requires you to choose the "larger" form of cooperation (Curry, Mullins and Whitehouse, *Is It Good To Cooperate, 50, fn 3.*). But the "larger" form of cooperation is a meaningless abstraction at best; at worst, it's a veiled form of "might makes right," where the lone individual dismisses his conscience to serve the interests and ensure the survival the larger group, or gang, or party, or state...

If morals are just tools of cooperation whose terms we can negotiate, they can lead people to some very unexpected places. There's no telling what man might give up when he's negotiating for his survival.

He might even give up his freedom.

Fyodor Dostoyevsky knew how it could happen. He was a novelist from Russia who was surrounded by people and raised in a culture that prized survival more than anything else. He wrote *The Brothers Karamazov*, which included an especially revealing and chilling scene in which a "Grand Inquisitor" hectors Jesus for burdening man with the ultimate freedom—to choose between good and evil—and making him responsible for his choices as he labors to create his world. "Never was there anything more unbearable to the human race," says the Grand Inquisitor, "than personal freedom!"[22] Nobody could have inflicted "greater perplexity and mental suffering than Thou has done," he says to Jesus, by troubling man's conscience "with so many cares and insoluble problems."[23]

Instead of giving man that freedom, the Grand Inquisitor says Jesus should have yielded to the temptations that Satan offered him in the desert so that he could satisfy man's longing to survive: He should have turned stone into bread to prove that he could feed man; he should have flung himself off the cliff to prove that God would always protect him; and he should have taken the throne as King of the Earth to prove to man that he was invincible. Jesus shouldn't have distracted man with questions of morality, says the Grand Inquisitor; instead, had Jesus reduced himself to a caretaker who believed that man *does* live by bread alone, man would rejoice at being "led once more like a herd of cattle."[24]

Abraham Lincoln said that the Russians "make no pretense of loving liberty" and their history supports what he said.[25] Maybe it was the brutal winters that made them covet survival above

---

22. Dostoyevsky, *Great Short Stories*, 239.
23. Dostoyevsky, *Great Short Stories*, 251.
24. Dostoyevsky, *Great Short Stories*, 260.
25. Basler, *The Collected Works*, Vol. 2, 323.

everything else; maybe it was because they were so vulnerable, situated on a vast open plain that Attila the Hun threatened, Genghis Khan conquered, and Napoleon and Hitler invaded. Maybe it was all those things and more.

Whatever the reasons, Russia is a telling example of the way people think and act when their survival is always top of mind. Yet this is the instinct to which Darwin appeals.

* * *

Darwin had one great idea—that all living creatures adapt and struggle to survive as they physically evolve—but he took it too far and claimed that it was behind everything man is and does. He wasn't content to simply let evolution be what it was (which as a scientific theory was grand enough) and his conceit led him to claim that it explained, not just man's physical development, but also his morality, sexuality, government and economics. And to this day his legions of followers continue to throw the evolutionary blanket over even more fields of endeavor, arguing that there's an ape in everything we do.

He thought his observations meant that man and animal were two of a kind, and that the story of man was just a struggle for survival—and he overplayed his hand. There's no doubt man wants to survive but he's motivated by other considerations as well, good and bad. By connecting morality to that one primitive desire, Darwin exposed *The Origin of the Species* to the same criticism that Huckleberry Finn had of *The Adventures of Tom Sawyer*: "It's mostly a true book," Huck said, "with some stretchers . . . ."[26]

Richard Dawkins wrote that the theory of evolution was special because it was "a powerful idea [that] assumes little to explain much."[27] Darwin's theory, he wrote, was "blindingly obvious" and "beguilingly simple."[28] But Dawkins said more than he knew; the theory of evolution blinded and beguiled Darwin into believing

---

26. Twain, *Adventures*, 5.
27. Dawkins, "*Matters*," para. 4.
28. Dawkins, "*Matters*," para. 1.

that it explained more than it did. It failed to explain (or simply ignored) the fact that man is so much more than a survivor. What other animal believes that it should:

"Love your enemies and pray for those who persecute you" (Matt 5:44 NIV).

"If your enemy is hungry, give him food to eat; if he is thirsty, give him water to drink" (Prov 25:21 NIV).

Or, gas the Jew and starve the kulak.

Man is a spiritual creature who's uniquely motivated by the desire to do good or evil. These are the codes that guide a transcendent being; they're the standards that he aspires to meet. By following them man has exposed the yawning chasm between the animal's struggle to survive and man's striving for God or descent into evil. Darwin said that the difference between man and animal is only one of degree and physically there's some truth to what he says, but in almost everything he does, man's spirit has distinguished him in a fundamental way.

Even something as pedestrian as an engineering project highlights the difference; a beaver dam and the Hoover Dam don't just differ in degree and neither do the creatures that made them. As physical structures they're roughly similar, but the purposes they serve are fundamentally different. One dam protects an animal and its kind from predators and gives them ready access to food; the other sustains life, yes, but it also includes a memorial to the 96 men who died creating a gigantic structure "to make the desert bloom."[29] They built it so the desert would bloom for an abundance of different species, not just man; and they built it so the desert would bloom for both the weak and the strong. It even sports an art deco design which has no implications for man's survival (and a debatable appeal to his appetite for beauty . . .).

The difference between animal and man manifests itself almost everywhere you look. And if you look you'll see that animals are merely survivors, but man is a survivor *and* a creator; and what he creates, as you'd expect, is simply a reflection of his soul's struggle with evil and good, and death and eternity.

29. Bureau of Reclamation, "Hoover Dam."

SCIENCE

* * *

There's another insidious aspect to the theory of evolution, at least if you swallow it whole; it'll dull your imagination, that faculty that Einstein said was more important than knowledge.

For proof we have Darwin himself. The contrast between him and Einstein is especially revealing. Whereas Einstein knew what he didn't know, marveled at the universe and upbraided the "fanatical atheists" who couldn't hear "the music of the spheres," Darwin's imagination waned as he came to believe that that his theory explained almost everything there is to know about man:

> Formerly I was led by feelings . . . to the firm conviction of the existence of God, and of the immortality of the soul. In my Journal I wrote that whilst standing in the midst of the grandeur of a Brazilian forest, 'it is not possible to give an adequate idea of the higher feelings of wonder, admiration, and devotion which fill and elevate the mind.' I well remember my conviction that there is more in man than the mere breath of his body. But now the grandest scenes would not cause any such convictions and feelings to rise in my mind.[30]

It's no wonder he felt that way. He was a tireless observer of nature and his sketches show how carefully he copied exactly what he saw, but he tended to see *only* the surface of things.

This was his habit of mind his whole life. He acknowledged his critics who said that he was "a good observer, but has no powers of reasoning,"[31] and he agreed with them that he excelled in "noticing things which easily escape attention, and in observing them carefully;"[32] he was proud of how hard he worked "in the observation and collection of facts."[33] And while he defended his ability to reason, he went on to indict the way he thinks in an

---

30. Barlow, *The Autobiography of Charles Darwin*, 91.
31. Barlow, *The Autobiography of Charles Darwin*, 140.
32. Barlow, *The Autobiography of Charles Darwin*, 141.
33. Barlow, *The Autobiography of Charles Darwin*, 141.

extraordinarily candid section of his autobiography that he called "an estimation of my mental powers."[34] He wrote,

- "My mind seems to have become a machine for grinding general laws out of large collections of facts."[35]
- "I cannot endure to read a line of poetry" and Shakespeare "nauseated me."[36]
- "I have almost lost any taste for pictures or music."[37]
- "I retain some taste for fine scenery, but it does not cause me the exquisite delight that it once did."[38]
- He admitted to "the atrophy" of that part of his brain "on which the higher tastes depend . . ."[39]
- "The loss of these tastes, is a loss of happiness, and may possibly be injurious to the intellect, and more probably to the moral character, by enfeebling the emotional part of our nature."[40]

This is the profile of a mind, not merely devoted to science, but in the grips of it.

When he was a young man he believed in God, but even his faith lacked nuance or depth and was based on a superficial reading of scripture. His belief, he wrote, was confined to the "the strict and literal truth of every word in the Bible" which he "did not then in the least doubt."[41] It was so much a part of his character that even his "orthodox" shipmates were amused by his facile reading of the Bible.[42] "I remember being heartily laughed at," he

---

34. Barlow, *The Autobiography of Charles Darwin*, 19.
35. Barlow, *The Autobiography of Charles Darwin*, 139.
36. Barlow, *The Autobiography of Charles Darwin*, 138.
37. Barlow, *The Autobiography of Charles Darwin*, 138.
38. Barlow, *The Autobiography of Charles Darwin*, 138.
39. Barlow, *The Autobiography of Charles Darwin*, 139.
40. Barlow, *The Autobiography of Charles Darwin*, 139.
41. Darwin, *The Life and Letters*, 45.
42. Barlow, *The Autobiography of Charles Darwin*, 85.

recalled, "for quoting the Bible as an unanswerable authority on some point of morality."[43]

One can only imagine how hard Darwin thumped the Bible to make nineteenth century orthodox Christians laugh at him. He must have delivered quite a sermon.

He may have understated things when he said that he was "quite orthodox"[44] when he was a young man, although he also said that "I do not think that the religious sentiment was ever strongly developed in me."[45] In any event, he seems to be the rare example of someone who, over the course of a lifetime, took the Bible and the world too literally.

* * *

The Origin of the Species was an unprecedented work of science but we'll have to look elsewhere for a better understanding of how and why human beings struggle.

More than 250 years before Darwin wrote *The Origin of the Species*, Shakespeare wrote *Hamlet, Prince of Denmark*. It's a story about a brutal fight for power within the court of a kingdom that's headed for war. As you read what happened to set the play in motion, ask yourself whether it's all just a clumsy and aberrant struggle for survival or something darker.

Before act one ends Hamlet sees the ghost of his dead father, who in life was the King of Denmark. The ghost tells him that Hamlet's uncle had poisoned him, a most "foul and unnatural" act.[46] Hamlet's uncle would eventually confess in a prayer that he murdered the king for "my crown, mine own ambition, and my queen," but in public he lies to the whole kingdom about what had happened, falsely claiming that a snakebite killed Hamlet's father;[47]

---

43. Barlow, *The Autobiography of Charles Darwin*, 85.
44. Barlow, *The Autobiography of Charles Darwin*, 85.
45. Barlow, *The Autobiography of Charles Darwin*, 91.
46. *Hamlet* (Bullen), 1.5.26.
47. *Hamlet* (Bullen), 3.3.55.

and Hamlet's mother quickly marries his uncle, the murderer, so her lust could "prey on garbage."[48]

It gets worse. Since Hamlet's father had been murdered while asleep in his orchard, there was no priest to administer last rites. The ghost of this Catholic king tells Hamlet that he was "cut off even in the blossoms of my sin;"[49] he said he was "doomed"[50] in purgatory "to fast in fires" until his sins were purged away.[51] The rules of the ghost's "prison house" forbade him from revealing what it's like, but if he could tell:[52]

> I could a tale unfold whose lightest word would harrow up thy soul, freeze thy young blood, make thy two eyes, like stars, start from their spheres, thy knotted and combined locks to part and each particular hair stand on end, like quills upon the fearful porcupine.[53]

For all of this, the ghost orders Hamlet to take revenge on his uncle.

His father murdered by his uncle and his mother corrupted by her lust—Hamlet's eyes were opened to evil. It all took place against the backdrop of war; Norway was preparing to invade Denmark and Hamlet's "seeming virtuous"[54] mother was really, as he put it, "the imperial jointress to this warlike state."[55] She and her new husband were struggling for their own survival and the survival of their kingdom, but much deeper currents were moving them too. And Hamlet knew it; regardless of the impending war with Norway, he recoiled at what they'd done and were planning to do.

Shakespeare's genius reveals so much more about man than Darwin's observations; he knew man had a soul. He knew man was both inspired by God and tempted by Satan so his characters

---

48. *Hamlet* (Bullen), 1.5.57.
49. *Hamlet* (Bullen), 1.5.75.
50. *Hamlet* (Bullen), 1.5.10.
51. *Hamlet* (Bullen), 1.5.11.
52. *Hamlet* (Bullen), 1.5.14.
53. *Hamlet* (Bullen), 1.5.15–20.
54. *Hamlet* (Bullen), 1.5.48.
55. *Hamlet* (Bullen), 1.2.9.

faced larger issues than mere survival. And he knew that when man descended into evil he wasn't kindred to an animal; he made himself lower than an animal. That's when man, Hamlet said in his despair, was no more than "the quintessence of dust."[56]

Darwin thought his theory would humble mankind. "Man in his arrogance thinks himself a great work," he said. "More humble, and I believe truer, to consider him created from animals."[57] And of course there can be no objection to being properly humbled whether you're a believer or an atheist. But Darwin didn't humble man; he degraded him.

* * *

Scientists have followed Darwin's lead and produced mountains of research on evolution, but the endless questions and answers that the theory of evolution entails, like all scientific inquiry, may fool them into believing that it can explain more than it does. The complexities of evolution are innumerable but it explains relatively little about man, and anyone who studies it with blinders on will suffer from knowing more and more about less and less. "A small circle," G.K. Chesterton wrote, "is quite as infinite as a large circle; but, though it is quite as infinite, it is not so large."[58]

These scientists' chosen field of study misses so much about the nature of man that it can mislead them into believing that there is no God or, if he exists, that he didn't give man a soul. If they think the theory of evolution disproves that God breathed life into man, then they need to free their curiosity to examine more than the common features of a man's hand and a bat's wing. And if that leads them to probe the mysterious depths of human nature and survey the incomprehensible breadth of human endeavors, then their reach will exceed their grasp and their imagination might come up with a surprising hypothesis to explain it all.

56. *Hamlet* (Bullen), 2.2.314.
57. De Beer, *Darwin's Notebooks*, 79.
58. Chesterton, *Orthodoxy*, 33.

Artists know that there's more to a creation than an image or likeness. "A painting is complete," Rembrandt is supposed to have said, "when it has the shadows of a god."[59]

So too, man.

---

59. The quote, while probably apocryphal, is certainly true.

III

Love

For Better or
For Worse

"You live once; you die once."—Salvo D'Acquisto

Thomas Aquinas defined love in one sentence. "To love," he said, "is to will the good of the other."[1]

His definition of love is simple and true. When you love someone you want what's best for him. You think about his welfare and then you act on it. True love is selfless.

Atheists and believers alike can accept Aquinas' definition of love, but here's the problem. What's simple and true isn't necessarily easy or even possible. How often do we love someone in a way that's unadulterated by any other considerations? When Paul elaborated on love in 1 Corinthians, he listed all of the things love is and isn't, and it seems like love is quite a chore. To truly love someone we must be patient, kind and rejoice in the truth; we mustn't be envious, proud, boastful, rude, selfish, or vindictive. And of course we also mustn't be quick to anger or delight in evil; instead, we should always protect, trust, hope and persevere (1 Cor 13:4–7 NIV).

---

1. Aquinas, *Summa*, I.II q 26 a 4.

"Love," Paul writes, "never fails" (1 Cor 13:8).

Paul's definition of love is essentially the same as Aquinas'—love is selfless—except that he lists all of the ways that love can go wrong and he shows how hard it is to love selflessly. It may be simply defined, but it isn't easy to do.

Here's another problem, a bigger one. Although you may love in a way that isn't flagrantly selfish, if you're honest with yourself you'll detect some selfishness in your motives, and maybe more than you'd like to admit. You want what's best for your spouse but you also know that your spouse makes money, satisfies your desires for sex and children, and provides some measure of regular companionship. You want what's best for your parents and siblings, but you also know that your parents protect and provide for you, and you have a bond with your siblings that you may need for support through hard times. You want what's best for your friend at work, but also you know that he's a part of your professional network, and his connections are a useful resource.

You may try to justify your selfish desires in any number of ways but they all usually make the same point: "I'm only human!" You may say, for example, that "there's nothing unnatural about me wanting sex and children, or relying on my family for support, or making progress in my career." And the only possible response would be, yes, there's nothing unnatural about it at all. These desires are part of your DNA and if they arise in your relationships to one degree or another, that doesn't that mean your love is hopelessly corrupt.

But it isn't selfless, either.

And our desires and regard for ourselves are probably more of a factor in our relationships than we like to think. We're quick to dismiss our mixed motives as unimportant and excusable, but we should pay attention to how other people feel to truly understand their significance.

How does a wife feel when she suspects that her husband's soothing words about something that upset her were chosen, at least in part, to end the conversation and put the matter behind them?

How does a father feel when he knows his daughter's exceptionally good behavior only coincides with her birthdays and Christmas?

How does a friend feel when he realizes that you lent an especially sympathetic ear to his worries about his child's health at the same time that you listed him as a reference for an upcoming interview?

These suspicions may or may not be well founded but they show how the slightest doubt about the purity of someone's love can spoil things. When we're on the receiving end at least, we are more apt to believe, as Shakespeare wrote, that "Love's not love when it's mingled with regards that stand aloof from the entire point."[2] And maybe this is why the Golden Rule—to love your neighbor as yourself—is a staple in all civilizations (it's found among the ancient Egyptians, Persians, Chinese, Greeks and Romans, and in Hinduism, Islam, Judaism and Christianity): Our instinct to love ourselves is so strong that we use it as a guide for how we should love others.

Pause for a moment and think about what that means. Our love for ourselves is so ingrained and steadfast that for thousands of years, civilization's greatest spiritual and secular leaders have used it to teach us how we should love others.

And there are other devices that we use to transcend our nature and love selflessly. The most common is marriage. When we marry we promise to love our betrothed even when there's nothing in it for us; we pledge our love all the same in sickness and in health, for richer or poorer. We make our promises in public; family and friends witness them, encouraging us to abide by our vows and deterring us from straying from them (or at least they're supposed to . . .). And the promises are binding until "death do you part"; marriage is a covenant, not a contract, the difference being that a covenant's terms can be accepted or rejected but never changed or negotiated.

2. King Lear (Bullen), 1.1.239–241.

We "tie the knot." Our nature demands it.

* * *

Less common are those who prove their love in situations where they not only have nothing to gain, they actually sacrifice and suffer for their beloved. These are heroes. They can come out of anywhere; they're all sorts of people, as different as can be . . .

There's Maximilian Kolbe, who was a friar in the Catholic Church in Poland. He helped to hide over 2000 Jews from the Gestapo and refused to cooperate with the Nazis who overran his country, so they imprisoned him in Auschwitz, the notorious concentration camp. When a prisoner escaped, the retribution was severe; Karl Fritzsch, the SS's deputy camp commander, picked ten men to be starved to death in an underground bunker.

One of the men he picked, Franciszek Gajowniczek, cried out, "My wife! My children!" That's when Kolbe summoned his courage and made the decision to martyr himself; he volunteered to take Gajowniczek's place. A janitor said the friar led all of the prisoners in prayer as they entered the bunker. He saw Kolbe and the others suffer in the following days. After two weeks without food and water all of the prisoners had died except for Kolbe, so the Nazis killed him with a lethal injection of carbolic acid.

Franciszek Gajowniczek lived to be ninety-four years old. He died in 1995.

There's John Fox, an African American soldier from Ohio who graduated with a degree in engineering from Wilberforce University after serving in the Reserve Officer Training Corps. He served in World War II with the segregated 92nd Infantry Division, which was attached to an artillery battalion to support the infantry. On the day after Christmas, 1944, he and a small party of soldiers volunteered to stay behind in Sommocolonia, a small Italian village from which American forces were retreating in the face of superior numbers of German soldiers. Fox hid in the second floor of a house.

LOVE

The Germans threatened to rout the Americans. Fox could have retreated but instead he radioed an order to fire heavy artillery on his own position because there were over one hundred German soldiers in the vicinity. The soldier who received the order was Fox's close friend, Otis Zachary; he was stunned and hesitated to follow it. "Fire it!" were Fox's last known words, and Zachary did just that when his superior officer told him to follow Fox's order.

The barrage killed scores of Nazis and allowed the Americans to safely retreat, avoid a rout, and organize a counterattack. They retook the village. That's where they found Fox's body in a pile of rubble.

There's Salvo D'Acquisto, born in 1920, the oldest of eight children in a working class family from Naples, Italy. He had a gentle disposition; a schoolmaster described him as "so quiet you would hardly think he was Neapolitan."[3] He showed how he cared for others at a very young age; villagers recalled how he'd given his shoes to a barefoot child he saw returning from school, and that he'd once saved a child from being run over by a train.

He was a policeman in Rome during World War II when Mussolini was deposed and the Italian government joined the allies. Italy's King Victor Emmanuel and senior military leaders fled Rome because the Germans advanced toward the city, but Salvo decided to remain at his post; he thought he could best serve the people in his town simply by being a policeman and maintaining order amidst the upheaval of war.

A couple of weeks after Mussolini was deposed, German soldiers were inspecting boxes of munitions that the Italian army had left behind in the Torre Di Palidoro, a medieval watchtower. There was an explosion, killing one of them. Without any evidence to support him, German Field Marshall Albert Kesselring assumed it was sabotage and, under a standing order for reprisal, he told his troops to round up and execute twenty-two civilians unless Salvo would investigate and identify the guilty party.

Salvo carefully examined the scene of the explosion and explained to the Nazis exactly how it had occurred and why it was an

---

3. Lucie-Smith, *"Incredible Sacrifice,"* para. 8.

accident, but to no avail; he was beaten, his uniform was torn, and twenty-two innocent civilians were forced to dig their own graves and face a firing squad beneath the medieval watchtower.

As Salvo watched the civilians dig their graves it was clear to him that the soldiers were going to follow through on their orders, so he interceded in the only way left to him; he confessed to a crime that he didn't commit. The Germans let their prisoners go and twenty-one of the twenty-two fled; only Angelo Amadio, a seventeen year old boy, remained behind to witness what happened. Earlier that day while the boy was digging his own grave, Salvo had told him, "You live once; you die once."[4]

Salvo liked to carry pictures of his girlfriend and the Sacred Heart wherever he went. "I'll keep both next to my heart," he'd written her.[5] The Sacred Heart is one of the most widely practiced devotions among Catholics, who believe that, among other things, it holds the promise that Jesus will be their refuge in death.

The Germans executed Salvo D'Aquisto September 23, 1943. He left twenty-two lives behind.

And there's Alfred Gwynne Vanderbilt. Born in 1877, he was the twice married heir to the Vanderbilt fortune and an alleged adulterer who enjoyed fox hunting and "coaching" (driving a coach through the toney neighborhoods of New York City and by quaint old inns in the English countryside). He was extremely wealthy, had a sharp eye for valuable real estate—and in 1915 he bought a first class ticket for himself and his personal valet aboard the RMS Lusitania.

It departed New York on May 1, bound for England; at 2:10 pm on May 7, German U Boat submarine captain Walther Schwieger ordered two torpedoes fired at the Lusitania, which was then ten miles off the coast of Ireland.

It took only eighteen minutes for the ship to sink because one of the torpedoes struck just below the ship's bridge, causing catastrophic structural damage. 1201 of the 1962 on board died. One of the survivors was Charlotte Pye, who grabbed her baby

---

4. Lucie-Smith, *"Incredible Sacrifice,"* para. 16.
5. Lucie-Smith, *"Incredible Sacrifice,"* para. 9.

Marjorie and ran onto the deck. The boat was listing and she saw "women shouting and screaming and praying to be saved."[6] One man, calm and resolute, came up to her and said, "Don't cry. It's quite all right."[7] Charlotte recognized him as Alfred Vanderbilt; just the night before he'd given her five dollars for a charity for which she was collecting donations.

He couldn't swim and it would have been impossible for her to stay afloat with a baby in her arms. He tried to find her a life jacket but there were none to spare, so he gave her his own. He tied it on her and helped her onto a lifeboat. Another survivor, Alice Lines, heard Vanderbilt tell his valet, "Find all the kiddies you can, boy."[8] As his valet brought them to him Vanderbilt "dashed to the boats with two little ones in his arms at a time." The ship's barber, Lott Gadd, later said in an interview that Vanderbilt was "trying to put life jackets on women and children. The ship was going down fast. When the sea reached them, they were washed away. I never saw Vanderbilt after that. All I saw in the water was children everywhere."[9]

His body was never recovered. A roadside memorial in England pays tribute to his sacrifice, noting that he was "a gallant gentleman."

* * *

They gave their lives for others, dying by a lethal injection, a military bombardment, a firing squad and in the icy waters of the north Atlantic. Strange as it sounds, they loved in the way that our marriage vows demand; they loved for better or for worse, except they did so for complete strangers. What motivated them to love selflessly, putting themselves aside and truly willing the good of the other?

Our hypothesis is, God's pure love and its influence over us.

6. Preston, *Lusitania*, ch. 17.
7. Preston, *Lusitania*, ch. 17.
8. Preston, *Lusitania*, ch. 17.
9. Preston, *Lusitania*, ch. 17.

God's patient and selfless love is a theme in almost every book of the Bible, starting with Genesis. After Adam and Eve succumbed to Satan's temptation and disobeyed God in their quest to "be like God," he could have damned them for eternity (Gen 3:4 NIV); rebelling against God is the ultimate crime deserving the ultimate punishment. Yet he withheld his judgment and instead expelled them from the Garden of Eden; in fact the story says that he was concerned enough about them that he even "made garments of skin . . . and clothed them" (Gen 3:21 NIV). He freed them, but he didn't abandon them even in the face of their conspiracy and rebellion.

God also made a hard decision that foreshadowed the difficulties to come. If he allowed Adam and Eve to return to Eden, he knew that their pride would lead them to disobey him again and "take also from the tree of life and eat, and live forever" (Gen 3:22 NIV). He didn't want them to spend eternity wrecked by pride and separated from him without any hope of reconciliation. So he decided to put "cherubim and a flaming sword flashing back and forth to guard the way to the tree of life" (Gen 3:24 NIV). They faced death and they could never return to Eden, but the door to reconciliation with him remained open.

We should take a moment to consider one of the most common and virulent objections that atheists make to the existence of God, which is based on their interpretation of the Old Testament. Atheists like to mock God because he smites empires and violently punishes humanity, but they should think about the nature of the crime that man committed when they judge the severity of the punishments that God imposed. Is it possible that a sentence can be severe and, at the same time, tempered by mercy and lighter than justice demands?

To see how this can be so, let's put God aside for a moment and focus strictly on your everyday relationships. When you disobey someone, the more authority he has, the more severely he'll punish you. Disobeying your older sibling is one thing; disobeying your parents is another. If you don't do what the team's captain wants you to do, you lose his confidence; if you don't do

LOVE

what the team's coach wants you to do, he cuts you. The principle extends all the way up to royalty; failing to obey a king can be treason, which is punishable by death.

Adam and Eve committed treason against God, and nothing less than treason. It happened in the Garden of Eden immediately after God had created them. And it wasn't merely *a* sin; it was *original* sin. It corrupted their nature and would corrupt all of their descendants, which is to say all of mankind. The depth and scope of this spiritual crime cannot be overstated. And yet for some reason, God didn't put an end to humanity right then and there. In fact, he allowed them to do as he'd originally commanded; they could be fruitful and multiply, which only broadened the scope of the conspiracy against him, increased the number of traitors by orders of magnitude, and tried his patience in more ways and to even greater degrees. Here we see the outlines of pure love, right at the beginning of the story of mankind.

Amidst all of the people and nations that God smites in the Old Testament, it's interesting that Adam and Eve are not among them; God could have condemned them to death, even before they stepped out of Eden. And yet he freed them to produce the human race.

When we read the Old Testament in the proper context, we see that God is remarkable, not because he punishes mankind and destroys empires, but because he allows them to exist in the first place.

And so the Bible is replete with examples of God's mercies, patient suffering and sacrifice. Chapter after chapter, book after book, the Old Testament tells how God repeatedly withholds his final judgment on his Chosen People despite their rank disobedience. His mercy for them is revealed in his message to Isaiah that "my unfailing love for you shall not be shaken" (Isaiah 54:10 NIV). And in the New Testament, the story continues and his love is expressed in a new and even more personal way, as Jesus bears and dies upon a cross to save us from ourselves.

His mercy and suffering for our sake shouldn't surprise us, not in the least; at a minimum, he's just following his nature. Since he's perfect, he has nothing to gain from mankind or anything else; God is the only being who, by his nature, can *only* love selflessly. Selfless love originated with him.

Following God's example, we strive to love selflessly despite what the world can do to us, and even in spite of ourselves. It is a type of love that Shakespeare describes most poignantly in *King Lear*. When the English king disowns his daughter, Cordelia, and warns her suitors that he won't provide a dowry, the Duke of Burgundy immediately loses interest but the King of France is steadfast in his devotion to her. Cordelia, he says, "is herself a dowry."[10]

In God's eyes, so are we.

There's a problem, however. If willing the good of the other is pure love, it seems like we cannot love God in return. What "good" can we possibly will for him? He's already perfect and lacks for nothing. It seems like loving God is like making a charitable contribution to a billionaire or teaching arithmetic to Einstein; it looks like an empty gesture, even an absurd one.

It's the point Job's accusers made to him. "Can a man be of benefit to God? Can even a wise person benefit Him? . . . What would He gain if your ways were blameless?" (Job 22:2–3 NIV)

Worse, if we can't love God then we can't form a bond with him. When we love someone we not only want what's good for him, we act on it; we share a piece of ourselves, say a thought or deed that our beloved needs. Then a bond is formed when we see ourselves, or a part of ourselves, in our beloved. "Love unites," Aquinas said, "by making what is loved as agreeable to the lover, as if it were himself or a part of himself."[11] However, there's nothing good that we can give to God that he doesn't already possess; there's nothing we can do to "make" him agreeable to us because he already is.

It seems like God's perfection is a blessing and a curse at the same time. Because he's perfect, he can want what's good for us and act on it; we, on the other hand, cannot conceive of anything that would be good for him, much less act upon it.

---

10. King Lear (Bullen), 1.1.242.
11. Aquinas, *Summa*, I.II q 28 a 1.

It looks like we're mismatched. It's a paradox, but if the old saw is right that a paradox is just a truth standing on its head for attention, then we should invest some time to figure it out.

With a little thought we can see that how we love him is different from how we love man. The unique way in which we do is suggested by how we love our superiors. Think of the troops who are devoted to an officer; or the players who believe in a coach; or the child who loves his parents. More than anything else, their superiors inspire them to become servants; the troops risk their lives for their comrades and cause; the players give it their all; and the children do their chores. They want what's best for their army, team or family (they will the good of the others); they give something of themselves to the people they serve (and see themselves as part of the army, team or family); and they wind up forming a bond with them.

In the same way, we draw inspiration from God and show our love for him by loving others. "Truly I tell you," said Jesus in one of his parables, "whatever you did for one of the least of these brothers and sisters of mine, you did for me" (Matt 25:40 NIV).

Think about Kolbe, Fox, D'Acquisto and Vanderbilt. They selflessly loved what God loved and became his servants. They answered the question that we thought was unanswerable—What good can we give to God? We give . . . ourselves.

This is how we form a bond with him. If we do his will and selflessly love what he loves (which includes all of God's children), he's more apt to say, that's *my* servant.

Must we sacrifice our lives in order to form a bond with him? Take heart; giving your life for someone else is the ultimate act of selfless love, but it's not the only way to love selflessly; in our everyday lives we can follow the Golden Rule, adhere to our marriage vows and treat anyone like they are "themselves a dowry." It's in a husband's show of affection "just because," or a kind word or patient ear for a stranger whose path we'll never cross again. You can even find it in secular culture's encouragement to practice "random acts of kindness" and to "be kind, because everyone you meet is fighting a battle you know nothing about." These examples of selfless love are still hard for us and the exception, not the rule, but they show that you don't have to be in a war zone or sinking ship to witness—or practice—them.

Whether it's heroic or common, true love is something special. It's like a miracle; just as God breaks the laws of nature when he performs a miracle, man acts contrary to his own nature when he loves selflessly.

The poet John Donne picked up on this theme. He worried that future ages would look for miracles in the wrong places; he rejected the idea that trinkets and baubles hold the power to work miracles—there are no "magic beans"—and instead focused on the human heart. So he wrote a poem about it, one in which a man describes his lifelong love for a woman:

> And since at such time miracles are sought,
>
> I would have that age by this paper taught
>
> What miracles we harmless lovers wrought.
>
> First, we lov'd well and faithfully . . . [12]

It's hard to say whether that's a miracle, something like a miracle or something else altogether, but by loving well and faithfully we take on the "shadows of a God" to some degree. Whether we paint ourselves the way Rembrandt would or some lesser artist depends on the circumstances and how we respond to them.

"Be perfect, therefore" the gospel according to Matthew says, "as your heavenly Father is perfect" (Matt 5:48 NIV).

It is a burden that's unique to God's children. A lioness may defend and care for her cubs because they'll strengthen the pride and increase her chances of survival; and a chimp may groom and cooperate with another member of his troop for the same reason. But unlike mankind, they don't sacrifice their lives for strangers or love selflessly in any way.

* * *

---

12. Donne, "The Relic," 151–152.

Now atheists will try to erase God from the picture by arguing that evolution proves that heroic acts of selfless love are unnatural and don't represent the true nature of man. Sacrificing your life or suffering for someone else, they may say, is so unusual that it's just an aberrant exception to human nature (like a mutation that doesn't support your own survival and therefore should disappear over time).

The argument doesn't wash. The heroic deeds of Kolbe, Fox, D'Acquisto and Vanderbilt (and many others, actually) may be unusual, but that doesn't mean they're unnatural. While it's certainly true that man rarely gives up his life for someone else, it's also true that he's rarely in circumstances where it's necessary.

They also claim that man's more common acts of selfless love can be easily explained by evolution and aren't really selfless. Compared to animals, they argue, man is more evolved; he can see further into the future. Caring for strangers, for example, may not benefit man immediately but he believes that it'll ultimately benefit him somewhere down the road.

The idea that we act selflessly because we believe it'll benefit us down the road sounds less like a scientific conclusion and more like a belief in karma, or a comforting but ridiculous belief that "good things happen to good people." When we're idling in traffic but stop anyway so a complete stranger can merge into our lane (just to take one ordinary example), do we really think that'll help our chances the next time we're in the other position? Atheists seem to think so, which makes for an interesting observation; as much as they pride themselves on being calculating and rational, so called "realists," atheists are very capable of taking a sentimental turn that distorts reality.

It's like they've listened to too much country music; add a fiddle and a steel guitar to their theory and you've got Clay Walker's *Chain of Love*. If you haven't heard it, here's what you've missed. It twangs about a fella named Joe who helps an old lady whose car had a flat tire. She reaches into her purse to repay his kindness but Joe will have none of it; he tells her to repay his kindness by doing a good deed for someone else. So the old lady drives off and stops to eat at a café where, inspired by Joe's example, she gives a one hundred dollar tip to a waitress who's pregnant and exhausted. Later that night the waitress goes home, curls up in bed and whispers to her husband that they'll be alright. And as it turns out, her husband is . . . Joe!

That's just not the way the world works and the Joes of the world know it. Songs and theories to the contrary only demean their sacrifice.

Man and animal are fundamentally different. Animals don't feel a limited obligation to their pack or herd because their instinct to survive is *less* evolved than man's; they behave that way because, unlike man, their instinct to survive is *fully* evolved but unopposed by God's call to love selflessly.

We, on the other hand, are called to "be perfect." For an idea of what that means remember where we began. Aquinas said that to love is to "will" the good of the other. At its core selfless love is a choice and like all choices, we're responsible for this one. Not only *can* we truly love someone by putting aside our own needs, even our own instinct to survive; we *must* put them aside—for better or for worse.

IV

Pride

Two Masters

"Every one of us . . . suffered from a peculiar duality of mind . . ."[1] —Nikolai Bukharin

"I stand on the threshold of my hour of death."[2] Nikolai Bukharin knew the court would convict him of treason and order his execution.

It was 1938 and Bukharin stood trial in communist Russia for conspiring to assassinate Vladimir Lenin, the godfather of the Russian revolution, and Josef Stalin, the dictator who inherited power from Lenin once the revolution was over. It was a baseless charge and everyone in the courtroom knew it.

The authorities also charged Bukharin with conspiring with other "wreckers" to dismantle what two decades of "socialist construction" had built. This too seemed like a baseless charge, especially since the real reason Bukharin was arrested had nothing to do with "wrecking" the cause of communism; he'd merely disagreed with Stalin about the best way to transform Russia's agricultural

---

1. Bukharin, "Moscow Trials."
2. Bukharin, "Moscow Trials."

economy into an industrial powerhouse, and that couldn't possibly be a threat to those two decades of supposed progress.

Or was it? It was a question that Bukharin asked himself, one that haunted him in the months leading up to his trial.

The issue was what to do about Russia's farmers. The wealthy ones, or "kulaks," sold their grain for profit and the peasants wanted to prosper like them. "Enrich yourselves!" Bukharin once told them, hoping they could be eased into socialism at a gradual pace.[3] But Lenin worried about how they wanted to become wealthy "continuously, daily, hourly, spontaneously and on a mass scale."[4] And Stalin was equally suspicious, never trusting them because they controlled the nation's food supply. Besides, he thought the peasants' labor would be better spent in manufacturing and similar industries.

So he confiscated the kulak's farms and forced many of the peasants to relocate and work in factories. The rest he left in the fields and drove like beasts of burden to produce enough food to feed the workers in the cities, allowing the peasants to keep very little for themselves. When Bukharin raised doubts about it and instead supported a slower and gentler approach, Stalin ordered his arrest.

Bukharin was the most prominent of seventeen defendants in the last of the Moscow "show trials," so called because they took place in front of the international media and featured "confessions" that were usually obtained through beatings and torture. Stalin orchestrated the trials because he wanted his countrymen and the world to see that his will was law. He always craved power and in the 1930s he found a ready pretext for crushing internal dissent and division; he knew that a clash with German, Italian and Japanese fascism was possible so he empowered himself to build "socialism in one country" and strengthen Russia. He hoped that the fascists would succumb to revolutions or the Russian military, clearing the way for communism to vanquish

---

3. Bukharin, "1925-N I Bukharin."
4. Lenin, "'Left Wing' Communism."

world's democracies where, he thought, capitalism was collapsing under the weight of the Great Depression.

Josef Stalin and a pivotal point in Russian history—the man and the moment—had met.

Stalin was determined that Russia would have the industrial might to fulfill its mission and he had the courage of his communist convictions to take power and make it so. He banished, jailed and executed political opponents like Bukharin. Their lives were trivial next to Russia's and communism's fate at such a critical time in history.

Imposing communist discipline on the countryside, and doing it without compromise, were also high on his agenda. And as a message to anyone who questioned his plan and the vigor with which he'd pursue it, he starved and executed the kulaks. Nobody knows for sure how many; it was at least 500,000, maybe millions. His zeal for communism and brutal implementation of it were unmatched.

As a young man in 1920s, Bukharin had promoted Stalin's rise to power, writing that "coercion, in all its forms, from executions to forced labor, is . . . the method of molding communist humanity."[5] At the same time, however, there was a hint of uneasiness in him; he'd also admitted that during the Russian civil war, he had seen terror and executions "that I would not want even my enemies to see".[6] And as the horrors multiplied under Stalin, Bukharin recoiled at the violence of it all, exposing him as someone who wavered between supporting violence in theory and opposing it in practice. When he visited Siberia in the 1930s and witnessed Stalin's abuse of the peasants, he had to be sedated.

Still his sympathy for the peasants only went so far; he believed in communism. Whatever misgivings he had about Stalin— he confided to an old adversary that Stalin "is not a man, but a devil"—he said he was nonetheless "the man to whom the party granted its confidence" and "a symbol of the Party."[7] Whenever he

5. Caute, *The Left*, 112.
6. Amis, *Koba*, 115.
7. Radzinsky, *Stalin*, 358.

criticized Stalin's abuse of the peasants as the editor of *Izvestia* (one of the state newspapers), he always did it indirectly and respectfully in order to maintain party unity.

In 1936 he visited Paris with his wife who was pregnant with their first child. He said to a friend, "Now [Stalin] is going to kill me," yet he refused to consider seeking asylum, telling his wife that he couldn't live outside of his native land.[8] Bukharin was Russian and in Russia, he wrote, "Three ethical norms dominate everything: devotion to the 'nation' or to the 'state,' 'loyalty to the Leader' and the 'spirit.'"[9]

His lively and accessible books on communist theory made him extremely popular in the party and around the country, but his revulsion for communist violence undercut his enthusiasm for the cause. His equivocation must have reminded his followers of the poem about the Duke of York and his ten thousand men . . .

> . . . He marched them up to the top of the hill,
>
> And he marched them down again.
>
> When they were up, they were up,
>
> And when they were down, they were down,
>
> And when they were only halfway up,
>
> They were neither up nor down.[10]

Stalin consistently demanded unqualified obedience. Bukharin responded by trying to find a middle ground between his sympathy for the peasant and kulak, and his belief in the historic mission of communist Russia. He tried being "neither up nor down." It was unsustainable.

It seemed like his trial would finally force him to take a stand; he could defend himself or confess to the charges. Not that it would matter in the end. He knew he'd be executed even if he denied the charges and proved that they were false. Stalin had coerced the

---

8. Liebich, "I Am The Last," 775.
9. Salisbury, "Bukharin and the Bolshevik Revolution," 15.
10. Opie, *The Oxford Dictionary*, 442-443.

other defendants and various witnesses to lie about his role in the supposed conspiracies. The outcome of Bukharin's trial was foreordained by a dictator who believed that justice and human lives were the collateral damage of his historic mission.

The choice that was left to Nicolai Bukharin was whether to die telling the truth or confessing to a lie. Bukharin decided to die telling the truth, or what he thought was the truth. It wasn't an attempt to find a middle ground; it signaled a final decision, once and for all, to either march up or down the hill.

He decided to make a last plea in which, yes, he'd refute the nonsense about conspiracies to assassinate Lenin and Stalin; he refused to confess to the crimes that he didn't commit (and in fact proved that they were false). But that wouldn't be his main point; he wouldn't mistake the props for the play. Instead he focused on the charge that he was a wrecker. And in open court in front of the international media, he confessed to it.

Bukharin was an intellectual and, unlike the other defendants, his confession was unusually thoughtful. While he certainly understood the implicit threat to his family based on how he might testify, there's no compelling evidence that he'd been beaten; to the contrary he was able to write four books while he was in prison, something that's almost impossible to do under severe physical and mental anguish. "I worked, studied," he said of his time in prison, "and retained my clarity of mind."[11]

It seems like he spent most of his time thinking. "I made a reevaluation of my entire past," he said.[12] Reflecting on what he'd done that made him a wrecker, he told the court that its "monstrousness . . . is immeasurable."[13] It convinced him of the "necessity to capitulate" and made him "bend my knees before the party and country."[14] His execution "would be justified," he said, "because a man deserves to be shot ten times over for such

---

11. Bukharin, "Moscow Trials."
12. Bukharin, "Moscow Trials."
13. Bukharin, "Moscow Trials."
14. Bukharin, "Moscow Trials."

crimes."[15] Ultimately he hoped his conviction and execution would serve as "the last severe lesson" for anyone thinking about doing what he did.[16]

The specific act that made him a wrecker was, simply, disagreeing with Stalin's decision to shoot and starve the kulaks, confiscate their farms, and enslave and relocate the peasants. Looking back on his career, Bukharin concluded that he'd become so engrossed in communist theory that he'd lost sight of a fundamental tenet of communist practice—that it was treason to disagree with the leader of the party.

It was something that was actually obvious, something he really couldn't deny. The conclusion was inescapable once three premises were established. First, as any communist who's studied his ideology knows, communism founded on the denial of the existence of God. It's something that its theorists and practitioners have admitted from its earliest days. Marx wrote that "communism begins from the outset with atheism."[17] Lenin followed up nicely, writing that "atheism is a natural and inseparable part of Marxism."[18] And their legions of followers have said the same thing so many times that atheism is widely accepted as the ideology's theoretical foundation and the practitioners' motivational force. Bukharin himself summed it up best. "In practice, no less than in theory," he wrote, "communism is incompatible with religious faith."[19]

Second, communists believed that they would liberate man from religious superstition by spreading scientific knowledge. "The general diffusion of scientific knowledge," Bukharin wrote, ". . . slowly but surely undermines the authority of religion."[20] Lenin believed it too, adding a thought about how the scientist and communist were natural allies; the "scientist," he argued, "must be a modern materialist, a conscious adherent of the

15. Bukharin, "Moscow Trials."
16. Bukharin, "Moscow Trials."
17. Marx, "Private Property."
18. Lenin, *Lenin Library*, 3.
19. Bukharin and Preobrazhensky, "The ABC."
20. Bukharin and Preobrazhensky, "The ABC."

materialism represented by Marx."[21] Together they would eradicate religion and everything else that they thought was irrational or superstitious. They even coined a new expression for what they would attack—they called it "false consciousness," which at least sounded like a clinical diagnosis that was based in science and logic. And so starting with faith in God and the dictates of conscience, and extending to emotional attachments to family and friends, they would replace the spiritual with the material; they'd replace God with science.

Finally, if man is just a physical or material thing like everything else in the universe, then the laws of nature dictate how he functions as surely as the laws of gravity dictate the movement of objects. Economics, politics and history are just as much sciences as chemistry, biology and physics. To communists like Bukharin, therefore, social science is the key to ruling and improving society.

This way of thinking explains the relationship between Stalin and Bukharin in particular, and between the communist and the people he rules generally. The communist is like a botanist or engineer, and people he rules are like plants in a garden or parts of a machine; they are objects that can be governed by scientific laws and, if necessary, subjected to scientific experiments. And just as the hedge doesn't decide where it should be planted and the part doesn't decide its function, the people don't get to decide their place and role in society. Therefore the kulaks' and peasants' desire for freedom was insubordination and anarchy, and Bukharin's support for them was treason. Dissent or "fractiousness" (as the communists called it) caused chaos and inefficiency, weakening Stalin, the party, and by extension all of Russia. Dissent *was* disloyalty.

Bukharin should have accepted the harsh facts that flow from those fundamental principles. He should have known that if there was no place for the kulaks, they would be discarded; and if the peasants were doing the wrong work in the wrong place, they would be relocated. And he should have known that his ideology required him to obey Stalin as automatically as energy and matter obey the laws of physics. Anything less, and he'd be a wrecker.

21. Lenin, "Significance."

As a believing if flawed communist to the end, Bukharin reflected on his dithering and he regretted it. In his testimony before the court he drew a sharp contrast between Stalin's wholehearted embrace of communism and his halfhearted efforts for the cause. There was Stalin, said Bukharin, "the hope of the world [and] a creator," standing at the forefront of "colossal socialist construction," a project that "advanced all the time very rapidly."[22] And there was Bukharin, hobbled by a "peculiar duality of mind";[23] if "I was sometimes carried away by the eulogies I wrote of socialist construction," he admitted, "on the morrow I repudiated this."[24]

Communism demanded too much from him. He and the other defendants withered in its shadow, leading to "a degeneration of ideas, a degeneration of psychology, a degeneration of ourselves."[25] He said it was "the catalytic agent" for the "the acceleration of the process of degeneration."[26] He didn't have the mettle to be a communist.

At the same time, Stalin and "the grandeur of socialist construction" was too powerful to resist.[27] It intimidated him, he said, so that he also suffered from an "incomplete faith in his counter-revolutionary cause," producing a "semi-paralysis of the will" and "retardation of reflexes."[28]

Those solitary months in prison had produced a revelation; the truth about himself was harsh. Bukharin wasn't strong enough to be a communist or to resist its savagery. Whether he was acting as a revolutionary builder or counterrevolutionary wrecker, he was guilty of communism's original sin; he was the one thing nobody could be and still survive in Stalin's Russia. He was, in a word, weak.

22. Bukharin, "Moscow Trials."
23. Bukharin, "Moscow Trials."
24. Bukharin, "Moscow Trials."
25. Bukharin, "Moscow Trials."
26. Bukharin, "Moscow Trials."
27. Bukharin, "Moscow Trials."
28. Bukharin, "Moscow Trials."

Bukharin learned too late that his disagreements with Stalin were understandable to an intellectual but unforgivable to a communist. When he advocated a mild and gradual transition to communism in the countryside, he stood as a roadblock in front of the Soviet Union's progress toward what he once called "the joy of the new life."[29] He became a "wrecker." Whatever Bukharin thought about Stalin and the peasants, a good communist would have known that it was trivial compared to the mission to march up the hill and defeat fascism and capitalism (and a careful reading of Bukharin's plea suggests that he thought even Stalin was too timid in fomenting communist revolutions in other countries).

All Stalin needed was a confession so he could get rid of a political opponent and strengthen his dictatorship; he saw Bukharin the same way that Caesar saw Crassus in Shakespeare's play: "He thinks too much," said Caesar. "Such men are dangerous."[30] But Bukharin gave Stalin more than he needed; while he proved that he wasn't involved in a conspiracy to assassinate Lenin and Stalin, he did admit that he had "endeavored to murder Lenin's cause."[31] It was more than a confession that he broke the law; it was a confession that he deserved to be executed.

In fact the contrast between him and Stalin was so sharp that he thought it wasn't even necessary for him to confess. Confession, he said, was an obsolete "medieval principle of jurisprudence."[32] His guilt was clear for all to see, a matter of simple observation, obvious and undeniable. The gap between Stalin's will and Bukharin's actions was that wide.

* * *

Why did he stray off course? His comrades always suspected he could be led by his feelings. Kliment Voroshilov, a fellow communist, sized him up in a speech before the party's central committee:

29. Bukharin, "Moscow Trials."
30. *Julius Caesar* (Bullen), 1.2.195.
31. Bukharin, "Moscow Trials."
32. Bukharin, "Moscow Trials."

> A word or two about Comrade Bukharin. . . . Why do I fear Bukharin? Because he is a soft-hearted person. Whether this is good or bad I do not know, but in our present situation this soft-heartedness is not needed. It is a poor assistant and advisor in matters of policy because it, this softheartedness, may undermine not only the soft-hearted person himself but also the party's cause. Bukharin is a very soft-hearted person.[33]

Stalin was there and commented about Bukharin, "Even now he is leading the retreat."[34] Lenin similarly demeaned him years earlier as "soft wax" on which "unprincipled persons can make an impression."[35] His flaw was a simple thing but devastating to the cause of communism—a feeling of sympathy (however modest it may be) for the peasant and kulak, maybe even a pang of conscience.

Neither the party nor Stalin would tolerate it. There was no place for feelings as far as they were concerned. Communism was based on reason and science; feelings were weakness and degeneracy, superstition and "false consciousness." An individual who allowed his feelings to compromise his devotion to the party had a criminal mind, which was worse than someone who merely didn't fit into a master plan, worse than waste or obsolescence. He was like a sprouting weed that had to be pulled or rusted gear that had to be replaced; he was a threat to the health and performance of everything around him.

Such was Bukharin. And coming at a turning point in history when the world was ripe for revolution but the Soviet Union was threatened by fascism, it was inexcusable.

So as the communists often put it, he had to be liquidated. He begged not to be executed the way so many others had been—by a gunshot to the back of the head. He wanted to die quietly, preferably by poison. But when the time came for his execution at the Kommunarka shooting ground, Stalin ordered his secret police to

---

33. Getty and Naumov, *Road to Terror*, 100.
34. Getty and Naumov, *Road to Terror*, 100.
35. Gregory, *Politics, Murder and Love*, 4.

make Bukharin sit in a chair and watch as they executed the other defendants, each by a gunshot to the back of the head. Then his turn came and he, too, died violently; the gunshot to the back of his head was the final message that he lacked the courage of his convictions and the willpower to be a communist.

Both in public and private, right up to the end, he'd expressed his belief in communism and his indifference to his own fate, the fate of the degenerate. He didn't want to live "isolated from everybody, an enemy of the people, in an inhuman condition, isolated from everything that constitutes the essence of life."[36] Beyond "everything positive that glistens in the Soviet Union" and the "reverberations of the broad international struggle," there was nothing, "an absolutely black vacuity."[37] He didn't have the strength to be a part of that struggle; he had no reason to live.

He'd told the court in his final plea, "What matters is not the personal feelings of a repentant enemy, but the flourishing progress of the U.S.S.R. and its international importance."[38]

He'd written his wife on the eve of trial, "Remember that the great cause of the U.S.S.R. lives on, and this is the most important thing. Personal fates are transitory and wretched by comparison."[39]

She wouldn't receive his letter until 1992, after the Soviet Union had collapsed.

The last time he'd seen Stalin was when he was arrested. "Friendship is friendship," Stalin told him, "but duty is duty."[40] In the end, Bukharin told the world that he agreed.

* * *

The arc of Bukharin's career is almost unbelievable. Once tagged by Lenin as "the favorite of the whole party" and its "most valuable and able theorist," he tirelessly labored to build a communist

---

36. Bukharin, "Moscow Trials."
37. Bukharin, "Moscow Trials."
38. Bukharin, "Moscow Trials."
39. Gregory, *Politics, Murder and Love*, 160.
40. Gregory, *Politics, Murder and Love*, 54.

society.⁴¹ Then he got in the way of a more ambitious builder and everything changed; suddenly his contributions looked feeble and his life became meaningless.

It was more than just another example of a revolution devouring its own; it was an example of a revolutionary who was content to be devoured.

Whittaker Chambers would have understood even though he landed in a different place. He was an American who spied for Russia until he had a change of heart and broke with communism permanently. He liked to explain what happened to him by telling a story that he'd heard from the daughter of a German diplomat in Moscow. Her father was a loyal communist, she said, until his entire outlook suddenly changed. She struggled to explain it, trying to find the right words. Then she said more than she knew. "One night, in Moscow," she said, "he heard screams. That's all. Simply one night, he heard screams."⁴²

Chambers said that every communist hears those screams. They either change him forever when he recognizes that they come from a child of God, an individual whose dignity dwarfs science, communism and the society they're supposed to produce. Or they're just noise that he dismisses while his calloused hands pull the levers of communism's brutal machinery.

Millions of people must have wondered whether anyone heard their loved ones' screams, people like Nadezhda Mandelstam. Her husband Osip, a poet, had written *Stalin Epigram*, a poem about Stalin and the climate of fear he'd created. "Every killing for him," the penultimate line went, "is delight."⁴³ Mandelstam read his poem to friends and colleagues in private, but someone gave the poem to Stalin; a few friends interceded on his behalf and Osip won a temporary reprieve, but inevitably he was arrested and sent to a prison camp, where he died a few months later. According to Nadezhda, the head of Stalin's secret police, Genrikh Yagoda, liked the poem and recited it to friends, but for him, just like for Stalin,

41. Salisbury, "Bukharin and the Bolshevik Revolution," 3.
42. Chambers, *Witness*, xliii.
43. Mandelstam, "Stalin Epigram," 47.

duty was duty. "For people of this extraordinary type," Osip's widow said, "human blood is like water."[44]

Early in his career, Bukharin wrote that the screams were necessary to mold communist humanity; midway through his career he witnessed executions in Siberia and had to be sedated; then, finally, at the end of his career and near the end of his life, he sat alone in his prison cell thinking about what he had lived for, and what he might die for.

At a minimum he knew what, or who, he *wouldn't* die for. After decades of equivocation he finally decided that his sympathy for the peasants and the kulaks was "false consciousness." True communists had no sympathy for them, much less a pang of conscience. He should have ignored their screams, he concluded, so in these last moments of his life, he expressed his indifference to their agony.

What *would* he die for? As he said in his confession, beyond the promise of the Soviet Union there was nothing else, an "absolutely black vacuity." So Bukharin defaulted to communism and the utopia it promised as his only option.

This ideology of his, however, was an odd one; it somehow justified his execution as an enemy of the people because he felt sympathy for millions of farmers. It couldn't have appealed to him like it once had. And in fact you can sense it in his confession and in his letters leading up to his execution; by comparison to his earlier writings, their tone is tepid and perfunctory as if he'd become more machine than man. His enthusiasm for the cause had declined; his party's voice had begun to sound strange and discordant but he continued to obey it because he couldn't find an alternative to the dictates of his ideology.

Bukharin was one of those communists that Whittaker Chambers described. There was no other voice, from without or within, that he would listen to; he ignored the screams and the pang of conscience.

* * *

---

44. Mandelstam, N., *Hope Against Hope*, 82.

How do you explain Bukharin, who once wanted to create the world anew, thoughtfully and deliberately condemning himself to empower a dictator?

Our hypothesis is, the existence of God and Satan, and the pride of mankind.

The Book of Genesis tells us a lot about God and Satan. It also tells us a lot about man, the creature who's caught in between them. And even though it was written thousands of years before the first communist revolution, it says a lot about oppression and freedom, Bukharin and Chambers, and just about everyone else.

We learn that God told Adam and Eve that they "must not eat from the tree of the knowledge of good and evil, for when you eat from it you will certainly die" (Gen 2:17 NIV). His command was simple and clear; he had no ulterior motive.

We also learn that Satan (in the form of a serpent) stoked Adam's and Eve's resentment of God's authority, cunningly suggesting that God's command limited their freedom more than it did. He asked Eve if God had forbidden them from eating the fruit of "any tree in the garden," when in fact he knew that God had told her not to eat the fruit of only one tree (Gen 3:1 NIV). Eve corrected him but the suggestion had its intended effect; she got resentful and, just like Satan, she exaggerated the constraints that God had placed upon her and Adam, complaining that God wouldn't even let them "touch" the forbidden fruit (Gen 3:2 NIV).

Then Satan stoked their pride, a much more dangerous temptation. He told them that they "will be like God" if they ate the forbidden fruit (Gen 3:5 NIV). This lie also had its intended effect; it made them believe that they could create their own paradise without the burden of obeying God.

Notice how Satan posed as a liberator, freeing Adam and Eve from the clutches of God so that they could be masters of their own destiny rather than submit to God's or anyone's authority. But as the story unfolds, Satan's ulterior motive becomes clear; Adam and Eve eat the forbidden fruit, God expels them from the Garden of Eden and, far from being like gods in an Eden of their own creation, they find themselves overwhelmed by a world of "thorns and thistles" (Gen 3:18 NIV).

They shunned him and relied on themselves; they got what they wanted but it didn't turn out as they expected; they separated themselves from God but they were hardly masters of their own destiny. And in fact after their allotted time passed, they both died just as God had warned them they would.

The Tree of Knowledge was the key that unlocked Adam's and Eve's pride and it's worth pausing to think about their motivation, what they experienced and how the Bible tells the story.

Their pride cannot be overstated; they wanted to be like gods. There were no limits to what they wanted to know; they wanted to know good and evil—and everything else.

The original Hebrew text makes this clear. When Eve looked at the tree she surmised that it was "desirable for gaining wisdom," but not just wisdom (Gen 3:6 NIV); the Hebrew word translated as wisdom, *śākal*, is translated elsewhere in the Bible as comprehension, discernment, expertise, attention, instruction, intelligence, prosperity, understanding, prudence and insight. Since Adam and Eve wanted to "be like god" and nothing less, it makes sense that they would want to know more than just morals, more than just good and evil, to fully comprehend everything about the world. They'd want everything expressed and implied by *śākal*; they'd want to know how the world works; they'd want to be omniscient to "be like god."

Likewise, the Hebrew word that's translated as "evil" in the Book of Genesis, *raʿ*, has a much broader meaning. The Bible translates it as trouble, harm, adversity, affliction and misfortune (and if used as an adjective it can be translated into another dozen or so words). The broadest translation of *raʿ* is, simply, "bad," and that best describes the vast scope of what Adam and Eve wanted to know, and what the fruit of tree was supposed to give them— the knowledge of "bad," which covers all kinds of problems, not just evils; it includes everything from disagreeable odors and unhealthy foods, to floods and diseases, to stubbing your toe or breaking your leg and all manner of accidents and misfortunes (we don't think of those things as evil because, unlike what human beings are capable of and sometimes do, they don't trouble us intentionally and maliciously).

The knowledge of all things good and bad would make them powerful, too, befitting the gods that they supposed themselves to be. They would know why something was bad and fix it; they'd use their knowledge to create a paradise that would rival the one from which God expelled them.

The story's rhetoric also suggests the unlimited scope of what Adam and Eve wanted to know. When it says that Adam and Eve ate from the Tree of the Knowledge of "Good and Bad," it's an example of what's called merismus, which is a way of describing the whole by contrasting its opposing parts. For example, instead of saying someone searched everywhere, we say that he searched "high and low" (the opposing parts of the search). In the same way, the author of Genesis describes Adam's and Eve's desire for omniscience by contrasting its opposing part—good and bad. In other words, we might say that Adam and Eve wanted their eyes opened to everything, "soup to nuts."

The depth of Adam's and Eve's pride is important because it explains a pattern of behavior that's repeated itself throughout human history. First man indulges his pride, believing that he has the knowledge and power to perfect himself and his environment; then man struggles and resorts to violence when he realizes that human nature and the world around him are at odds with his pretensions; and, finally, he destroys himself and his world, revealing his foolishness.

"Pride goes before destruction," says Proverbs 16:18, "a haughty spirit before a fall." It's the story of Bukharin and communism and many of the world's tyrannies. It's also the story of every man, woman and child on earth, although it's always an open issue whether we break free from the pattern like Chambers or succumb to it like Bukharin. The story shows that human nature hasn't changed over the eons; all that's changed are the names, especially the names of those who play the role of the serpent.

PRIDE

It's easiest to see the pattern by listening to the tyrants themselves because, for some reason, they are surprisingly candid about who they think they are and what they plan to do. They're nothing if not proud and they don't hide their ambitions to create a new man and a new world. Here's what a few of them have said about what they plan to do and the violence they'll use against anyone who stands in their way (some of their words are in italics to emphasize what they all have in common):

* * *

A terrorist, said the Ayatollah Khomeini, the Shiite cleric who led the revolution to make Iran a theocracy, must "wage war until *all* corruption, *all* disobedience of Islamic law *ceases*."[45] He and his fellow clerics "want to implement a policy to *purify* society."[46] Decades after Khomeini died, Abu Bakr al-Baghdadi, the Sunni leader of the Islamic State, had the same ambitions for the Muslim and the world he lives in. He said that "soon ... a day will come when the Muslim will walk *everywhere* as *master*, having honor, being revered, with *his head held high*, and his dignity preserved."[47] He wanted the world to know that "we are living today in a *new era*."[48]

And how will Muslims and their society reach such heights? Al-Baghdadi put it simply. Islam, he said, is "the religion of *fighting*."[49] Khomeini was just as clear but more dramatic. "The *sword*," he told his masses of followers, "is the key to *paradise*."[50] He said "It is Allah who puts the gun in our hands."[51] War, he said, "is a blessing for the world and for every nation."[52] He said that establishing "the Islamic state *world-wide*" was one of "the

---

45. Landes, *Heaven on Earth*, 446.
46. New York Times, *Interview*, 35.
47. Dabiq, *Just Terror*, 2–3.
48. Dabiq, *Just Terror*, 2–3.
49. BBC News, *Islamic State*, 13.
50. Khomeini, "Islam," 32.
51. Landes, *Heaven on Earth*, 446.
52. Landes, *Heaven on Earth*, 446.

great goals of the revolution."⁵³ If that seems wrong to anyone, it's because they're ignorant of the meaning of a holy war; students of Jihād, Khomeini wrote, "understand why Islam wants to conquer the whole world."⁵⁴ After defeating Iraq in a war that was raging at the time, he promised them that "we shall turn to other wars" because "a *religion without war* is a *crippled* religion."⁵⁵ He wanted every Muslim to know that "to *kill the infidels* is one of the noblest missions Allah has reserved for mankind."⁵⁶ Until the day comes when "the cry 'There is no god but Allah' resounds over the *whole world*, there will be *struggle*."⁵⁷

* * *

Fascism, Hitler said, "is the determination to create a *new man*."⁵⁸ Fascists must "set *race* in the *center of all life*" and they must "keep it *pure*."⁵⁹ He wrote that if Germany dedicated itself "to the care of its best racial elements, [it] must someday become *Lord of the earth*."⁶⁰ Hitler's minister of propaganda, Joseph Goebbels, hinted at what that meant. "We must have a *healthy people* in order *to prevail in the world*," he said.⁶¹ "We do not subscribe to the view that one should feed the hungry, give drink to the thirsty or clothe the naked . . . Our objectives are *entirely different*."⁶²

If the race must be kept pure then there are two types of people who are a threat to it. First and most obviously, there's everyone who isn't one of the master race. In Hitler's autobiography and manifesto, Mein Kampf, he spoke his mind about inferior

53. Bonney, *Jihād*, 251.
54. Khomeini, "Islam," 32.
55. Landes, *Heaven on Earth*, 446.
56. Landes, *Heaven on Earth*, 446.
57. Wright, *The Last Great Revolution*, 66.
58. Fest, *Hitler*, 533.
59. Hitler, *Mein Kampf*, 403.
60. Hitler, *Mein Kampf*, 688.
61. Burleigh and Wippermann, *The Racial State*, 69.
62. Burleigh and Wippermann, *The Racial State*, 69.

races to the 5,200,000 people who bought his book in any one of the eleven languages into which it was translated. "All who are not of good race in this world," he wrote, "are *chaff*."[63] Since that's a lot of people, the majority of people in the world in fact, that means that their existence and potential for mixing with the master race was a massive threat to its purity, which points to the second type of people who were part of that threat—those who were unwilling or unable to fight and kill for it. Here again Hitler was clear. Mein Kampf means "*My Struggle*" and it left no doubt that his beliefs would be spread through violence. Hitler wrote that "*he who would live must fight*" and that protecting the purity of the race "must necessarily be a *bloody* process."[64] As his own threat to anyone who thought differently he followed his argument to its logical conclusion, writing that "he who doesn't wish to fight in this world, where *permanent struggle* is the law of life, has not the right to *exist*."[65]

* * *

Writing about the promise of communism, Leon Trotsky said "Man will make it his purpose to *master* his own *feelings*, to *raise* his instincts to the heights of *consciousness* . . . to create a *higher biological type*, or, if you please, a *superman*."[66] The key, he said, was to "supplant mysticism by *materialism*, broadening above all the collective *experience* of the masses . . . [and] widening the horizon of their *positive knowledge*."[67] His stated goal was nothing less than "the *abolition* of earthly chaos."[68] Bukharin had the same ambitions. In a communist society, he said, "there will no longer be *anything* mysterious, incomprehensible, or unexpected."[69]

63. Hitler, *Mein Kampf*, 296.
64. Hitler, *Mein Kampf*, 333.
65. Hitler, *Mein Kampf*, 221.
66. Trotsky, *Literature and Revolution*, 207.
67. Trotsky, "Antireligious Propaganda," para. 3.
68. Trotsky, "Antireligious Propaganda," para. 17.
69. Laski, *Communism*, 160.

And Friedrich Engels, who wrote The Communist Manifesto with Marx, said exactly the same thing. By using science, he said, "the *whole sphere* of the conditions of life which surround men ... now comes under the dominion and conscious control of men, who become for the first time the real, conscious *lords of nature*."[70] Men will be "*master* of their own social organization."[71]

Since we know Bukharin's fate and something about Stalin's brutality, it's not hard to figure out where all this talk led. While nobody in the history of communist Russia matched Stalin's record for violence and murder, nobody justified violence and murder quite like Lenin. Communists, he said, must never forget that "the *class struggle* assumes the form of *armed conflict* and civil war."[72] At times, he wrote, it calls for "*ruthless extermination* of its enemies in open armed clashes."[73] The revolutions to create communist societies would be especially violent, as would the measures to sustain them after the revolutions were completed. Five years after the communists took power in Russia, Lenin wrote that communists must:

> carry out the confiscation of church valuables with the most savage and merciless energy.... Precisely at this moment we must give battle to [the clergy] in the most decisive and merciless manner and crush its resistance with such brutality that it will not forget it for decades to come.... The greater number of representatives of the reactionary clergy and reactionary bourgeoisie we succeed in executing for this reason, the better.[74]

To preserve "the Soviet government" and the "new order of life," communists must "stand for *organized terror*," Lenin said. "This should be frankly admitted."[75] Trotsky summed it up well, writing that he and his fellow communists "must rid ourselves once

70. Raico, *Great Wars*, 145.
71. Raico, *Great Wars*, 145.
72. Ryan, *Lenin's Terror*, 48.
73. Ryan, *Lenin's Terror*, 48.
74. Amis, "Deadly Revolution," 3.
75. Midlarsky, *Origins*, 127.

PRIDE

and for all of the Quaker-Papist babble about the sanctity of human life."[76]

These tyrants like to claim that their visions are unique but they are all rooted in the same desire. They want to assume the role of the Creator, forge a new man and turn the world into the warped paradise of their imagination. And they spread that desire as far and wide as they can; when you listen to what they say, you see how they craft their messages to swell the pride in their followers, blinding them to the absurdity of their wild ambitions. They also like to portray themselves as indispensable to the fulfillment of their visions, which means that strict obedience to their will is necessary to build the world that they've imagined.

They're like professional magicians; they just use different props. The communist uses science, the fascist uses race and the terrorist uses religion. But they all conjure the same illusions that the tyrants themselves describe in almost identical terms: Pure races and pure societies . . . new men and new eras . . . lords of the earth and of nature . . . masters and supermen. These messages are neither unique nor unprecedented; they're just echoes of Satan's ancient promise, "And ye shall be as gods."

And in their quest to displace God and create man and his world anew, they all agree and are strikingly honest about how they'll achieve their goals. "The sword is the key to paradise." . . . "[It] must necessarily be a bloody process." . . . "We stand for organized terror." Peel back the different histories, cultures and languages, and underneath you find humanity all the same, still plagued by original sin.

Nikolai Bukharin rejected God and made science the center of his world. Justice was harsh for him and for communism just like it was for Hitler and fascism, and in time it may turn out the same way for myriad terrorists and their ruthless theocracies.

"Do not worship any other god: for the Lord . . . is a jealous God" (Exod 34:14 NIV). It's sound advice. Atheists often say that

---

76. Amis, "Deadly Revolution," 13. Stalin certainly agreed; he murdered millions in Russia, in Europe and even in far flung places like Mexico, where his agents axed Trotsky to death.

a jealous God is a petty and arbitrary God, one that's hard to take seriously. Certainly human jealousy can be those things, but God's jealousy is different. It isn't wasted on small things; it's reserved for the things that take us away from him, things that can destroy us. This jealous God is worth taking seriously.

* * *

We're nothing like Khomeini, Hitler or Stalin of course, but in our private lives we are subject to the same temptations that they felt and we're just as capable of succumbing to them. Do you know anyone, for example, who browbeats his children with an especially harsh and unforgiving moral code, demanding that they be pure and righteous and showing them what Shakespeare called "the steep and thorny way to heaven"?[77]

Do you know anyone who makes race the center of his life, constantly pointing out the successes of those who share his heritage and blaming all of his problems on what he dismisses as the chaff of the world?

Do you know anyone who wants to plan and control what you do, maybe a boss who meddles in every decision you make or a neighbor who calls the homeowners association whenever he spots anyone doing anything that detracts from his vision of an ideal neighborhood?

What would these people do if they had the power of dictators or revolutionsaries?

We like to complain that we lack the clout to create the world that we want, but as Thomas Gray wrote in his *Elegy Written in a Country Churchyard*, it may be better that we live modestly with our . . .

> . . . crimes confined;
>
> Forbade to wade through slaughter to a throne
>
> And shut the gates of mercy on mankind.[78]

---

77. *Hamlet* (Bullen) 1.3.48.
78. Gray, "Elegy," 329.

Gray's *Elegy* is a sober reminder to be careful what you ask for.

Just because you wield less influence than dictators and revolutionaries, however, doesn't mean there's less at stake. Even if you aren't caught up in the intrigue of politics, revolutions and wars, your power over others, and their power over you, deserve your unflinching scrutiny. What you learn may not affect the destiny of nations but it will reveal something about your soul.

Adam and Eve separated themselves from God as they began their lives together. Shortly before he was executed, Nikolai Bukharin did the same. Most of us are "midway along the journey of our life" like the pilgrim in Dante's *Divine Comedy*, except that he got to explore paradise where God lives with his children, and the inferno where the damned have separated themselves from God.[79] We don't have Dante's imagination (and nobody reads *The Divine Comedy* nowadays) so we don't see those destinations very clearly. As a result we're more prone to wander from one path to the other without thinking about where either one leads.

We have to choose. Are we hobbled by a "peculiar duality of mind"? If so, we may be more like Bukharin than we think. His downfall proved the foolishness of trying to serve two masters; the consequences of doing so can be severe here on earth but they'll be irreversible hereafter, where we'll only serve one.

---

79. Alighieri, *Divine Comedy*, 67.

V

Suffering

Thorns and Thistles

"My old Father used to have a saying that 'If you make a bad bargain, hug it the tighter.'"[1]—Abraham Lincoln

There are two adages that people like to quote to those who are suffering. One says that "God won't give you more than you can handle." The other says that "What doesn't kill you makes you stronger." One's religious and the other's secular but they both say the same thing; they're messages of hope that are intended to buoy the spirits of someone who's hurting.

And they have something else in common too; they're not true.

Paul's first letter to the Corinthians supposedly supports the idea that God won't give you more than you can handle, but we're misreading those passages when we interpret them that way. Paul writes that God won't give you greater *temptation* than you can handle, not suffering: "No temptation has overtaken you except what is common to mankind," he wrote (1 Corinthians 10:13 NIV). "And God is faithful; He will not let you be tempted beyond what you can

---

1. Burlingame, *Abraham Lincoln*, 189.

bear. But when you are tempted, He will also provide the way out so that you can endure it" (1 Corinthians 10:13 NIV).

The Greek word that's translated as temptation, *peirasmos*, can also mean suffering but the context of Paul's letter shows he was talking only about the temptation to sin. The verses leading up to verse thirteen make this clear. They're all about avoiding a variety of temptations, from "setting our hearts on evil" and acting like "idolaters" who "indulge in revelry" and "sexual immorality"; to admonitions that "we should not test Christ" and should not "grumble" (1 Corinthians 10:7–10).

Paul is saying that we can resist temptation but that doesn't mean that we'll never suffer beyond our capacity to cope. In fact, by resisting temptation we may bring terrible suffering upon ourselves, even more than we can handle. Resisting the temptation to lie, for example, may mean confessing to a crime and going to prison; resisting the temptation to cowardice may mean going to war and sacrificing your physical or mental health, or even your life.

It's strange that any verse that Paul wrote would be interpreted that way because in his second letter to the Corinthians, Paul admits his own inability to cope with the suffering that he had to endure. Paul and his friends, he wrote, were "under great pressure, far beyond our ability to endure, so that we despaired of life itself" (2 Corinthians 1:8 NIV). They "felt we had received the sentence of death" (2 Corinthians 1:9 NIV).

Eventually Paul found hope even though God had given him more than he could handle. His suffering happened, he said, "that we might not rely on ourselves, but on God who raises the dead" (2 Corinthians 1:9 NIV). Ultimately, after listing all of the ways in which he'd suffered he contrasted God's power with his own weakness and, in a manner that was so characteristic of Paul, he celebrated his humility. "If I must boast," he wrote, "I will boast of the things that show my weakness" (2 Corinthians 11:30 NIV).

We're no better off believing that what doesn't kill us will make us stronger. How often the opposite is true. Think of the women who have been betrayed by their faithless husbands and left alone with broken families to fend for themselves and raise their children.

Think of the parents who've lost a son to an addiction that inexorably destroyed his mind and body, leaving them with a hole in their lives that will never be filled. Think of the men who've worked decades of physical labor, only to retire bent and feeble. The fact is, in so many ways, what doesn't kill us makes us weaker.

We probably cling to these adages, false though they are, not because they comfort the afflicted but because they comfort us. None of us wants to suffer and it's soothing to think that no matter what happens to us or our loved ones, we can handle it and, if we survive, we'll emerge even stronger.

This is the message of prosperity preachers and motivational speakers; they inspire their rapt audiences by creating the illusion that anyone can prevent or conquer suffering by changing his way of thinking. Neither of them preach Christ crucified (although only one of them may be excused for not doing so . . .), and the spell they weave typically starts to dissipate the next morning when their flocks leave for work or struggle to get the kids off to school. They either realize that they've wasted their time on someone who's given them a bucket of attitudes to adjust, all with the same prospect for success as their New Year's resolutions; or they return the following week to their church pews and conference centers to escape reality again.

We need to face what suffering is. The word suffer comes from the Latin *suffere*, which means to bear, undergo or endure. Suffering is not a problem to be solved, an error to be corrected or a challenge to be met. It's possible to overcome all of those obstacles, and facing them with imagination and a heart full of hope can help you do it. Suffering, however, is much more serious and powerful; it must be borne and endured until it departs on its own (or takes you with it). The truth is harsh: "[T]here is nothing we can do with suffering," wrote C.S. Lewis, "except to suffer it."[2]

Another reason suffering vexes us, believers and atheists alike, is that it strikes randomly and afflicts people to wildly varying degrees. The gospel of Luke tells the story of two events in Galilee, one when Roman soldiers slaughtered innocent pilgrims and the other

---

2. Lewis, *Grief*, 33.

when a large tower collapsed on unsuspecting bystanders (Luke 13:1–5 NIV). The soldiers intentionally killed the pilgrims and the bystanders died by accident, but both sets of victims suffered arbitrarily and severely. It made no sense, just like so much of the suffering that we witness and experience makes no sense.

Random suffering is especially cruel when it afflicts us and spares people who are guilty of any number of sins or vices. Psalm 73:13–16 says what we've all felt:

> Surely in vain have kept my heart pure and have washed my hands in innocence. All day long I have been afflicted, and every morning brings new punishments. . . . When I tried to understand all this, it troubled me deeply.

"Some rise by sin," Shakespeare observed, "and some by virtue fall."[3] It's a fact that makes believers and atheists ask the same question: "Where's God amidst all this suffering?"

Some believers have tried to reconcile human suffering with God's love by telling themselves that those who are suffering must have failed God in some way. It's the implicit message of prosperity preachers; after all, if believing will improve your fortunes, it follows that your misfortunes must be a result of your lack of faith. It's a dark and shameful message but it sells well, especially if you aren't suffering. It makes you feel like your situation in life is a sign of God's approval. It makes you feel righteous.

It's no wonder that these preachers sell tens of thousands of books and fill arenas and stadiums with their faithful. They don't call sinners to repent; they throw a party for the righteous.

There's an ever darker side to this way of thinking, however. It leads you to believe that, unlike you and your friends, whoever is suffering has secretly committed some sort of sin or crime, something that nobody knows about yet. It excites your imagination and makes you assume the worst. So when your neighbor is suffering, you draw the blinds and turn away.

There's no use assuming someone's guilty just because they're suffering some misfortune. The country music legend

---

3. *Measure for Measure* (Bullen), 2.1.41.

Hank Williams, who also had a little blues in his soul, asked the right question:

> Somebody that fell, he's the same man as before he fell, ain't he? Got the same blood in his veins. How can he be such a nice guy when he's got it and such a bad guy when he ain't got nothin'. Can you tell me?[4]

Jesus addressed the issue in a similar way, but he went a little further. When he talked about what happened in Galilee, he didn't just talk about the people who died. He talked about all of us. And it wasn't comforting. "Do you think that these Galileans," he asked, "were worse sinners than all the other Galileans because they suffered this way? I tell you, no!" (Luke 13:3 NIV) He told us that we're all guilty of sin; it's just that some of us haven't suffered for it (at least not yet). He seemed to be saying that we shouldn't see the dead as guilty and unfortunate; we should see ourselves as guilty and blessed.

It may seem to be an unduly harsh judgment but that depends on your perspective. Imagine two high school basketball players who are about play a game of one on one. They're both good athletes, both starters on their team. One of them plays at a level above the other, however, and he wins the game. As they walk off the court, the loser is spent and sore but the winner feels refreshed as if the game was nothing more than a healthy workout. And just when he starts strutting and trash talking, out of nowhere Michael Jordan walks onto the court and says, "Hey boys, let's play, me against both of you."

They accept the challenge, Jordan runs circles around them and when that game ends, Jordan's the one who hasn't broken a sweat but the high school players, both of them, are spent and sore.

How Michael Jordan judges our basketball skills—and how God judges our righteousness—differ from our judgments of "winners" and "losers." The winners look a little less like winners.

So we suffer, maybe a little more humbly than before we considered God's perspective, but we suffer nonetheless. It begs the

---

4. Escot, *Hank Williams*, chapter 10.

question, How can a loving God allow us to suffer, especially when suffering afflicts people so randomly and to arbitrary degrees? Atheists ask this question all the time because they believe that suffering disproves the existence of God (or at least of a loving God).

Our response and our thesis is that a loving God must allow man to suffer, even in random and arbitrary ways.

To see why this is so, first we have to identify the cause of human suffering, which is God's gift of free will; it explains all of the suffering in the world in some obvious and not so obvious ways.

When God gave man his freedom, it meant he could intentionally harm someone else or even himself. It's something we see all the time in big ways and small. A dictator murders millions of victims and descends into a bunker to commit suicide; a jealous man punches the rival for his girlfriend's affection and drinks to excess in despair over her choice. The connection between free will and human suffering is obvious and direct when man intentionally hurts himself or someone else.

There are other causes of suffering, however, in which man's free will doesn't seem to play a part. We suffer from natural disasters like earthquakes and floods, and millions have died from pandemics and diseases. What does free will have to do with any of these afflictions? No child chooses to die from leukemia; no family chooses to perish in a flood; nobody has the power and chooses to afflict others in these ways. And then there are human errors and ignorance, those destructive mistakes that can cause pain and cost lives. Nobody chooses to drop a box on someone else's foot or get into an automobile accident. Free will doesn't seem to explain any of this suffering.

A careful reading of the Bible, however, explains the connection between free will and the hardships and agonies that nature and man haphazardly inflict upon us. It's not obvious because unlike the situations in which man intentionally does evil, the connection is indirect but it's there nonetheless.

To understand it, it's important that we begin at the beginning.

The Creator knows how his creation works, so Adam and Eve had to obey God to live in harmony with the rest of his creation.

And in fact before the fall, in the brief period of time between man's arrival in Eden and his expulsion from it, there was no violence or conflict; man did not suffer or die.

But as the story goes, Adam and Eve chose to disobey God. They ate the fruit that Satan said would liberate them from God; it would give them wisdom so they no longer would have to rely on him; instead, they would be as gods and rely on themselves.

So they disobeyed him, he expelled them from Eden and sent them into a world of "thorns and thistles." This world was unique and was perfectly suited for a being who wanted to divorce himself from his Creator, but whose Creator still loved him. It was a place where God loosened his grip on things, without completely letting go and abandoning man. As a result, his creation unraveled a bit but it didn't become completely unspun.

It was a place where man could make his own way without ever fully understanding or controlling it. This world of thorns and thistles would always feel a little strange to him, and he would always be a little unsure of himself. Now man could enjoy a secure environment or suffer in a natural disaster; he could be healthy or sick. It was a world in which he would live, and die.

Man, in his pride, thought at first that he was smart enough to understand and powerful enough to control what God had created, but when God loosened his grip he quickly realized that he didn't have sufficient knowledge or power to make up the deficit. He tried; he made progress; he always came up short.

He learned a harsh lesson. He couldn't replace God. He wasn't the Creator.

The Creator knows how his creation works.

Even when he made progress, his work was always a mixed bag. The moment Adam assumed the role of creator and started providing for himself, things looked . . . different. He fed and clothed himself but he slaughtered animals to do it. He tilled the soil but axed trees and uprooted flowers and pastures in the process, destroying the habitats of myriad animals, insects and vegetation; and he yoked beasts of burden to plow fields (foreshadowing Dr. Frankenstein, who confessed that he "tortured the living animal to

SUFFERING

animate the lifeless clay."").[5] Adam learned by the sweat of his brow that life apart from God was harder than he'd expected.

The progress he made always came at a cost and the story continues today. Man struggles to remove a thorn from his life but frequently exhibits a clumsiness and brutality that creates another thistle. Woman brings life into the world but weakens herself in the process; man lives comfortably in a world he's depleted and polluted. It's something that we often overlook because we think it's unimportant (until we're pricked by the thistle later on).

In man's effort to tame a hostile world, sometimes he's inflicted a lot of collateral damage. In a sense, for as long as he's existed, man's played with fire; there's always been something dangerous about him. He's like a child behind the wheel of a Corvette; what began with a thrill when he took the keys, became terrifying when he started down the road. At his worst he's like a talented apprentice who refuses to listen to his master and sets the shop on fire. Macbeth, who was as bloodthirsty as any of Shakespeare's villains, is an extreme example of how man can make things worse even when he's fraught with guilt over what he's done. The whole ocean, he said, couldn't wash the blood from his hands; rather, his hands would "the multitudinous seas incarnadine."[6]

Right up to the present day man's ignorance and weakness don't just affect his actions; they often make him incapable of acting. There are thorns and thistles that he can't see, making him completely vulnerable to them. Wildfires and floods, children afflicted with leukemia and the elderly afflicted with Alzheimer's, or the blister that killed Theodore Roosevelt's son because it got infected before man discovered penicillin—we always seem to be on the brink of a secure existence independent of God until we're blindsided again.

This world of thorns and thistles sent a clear and painful message that man didn't have what it takes to replace God. Job learned this lesson, which is among the hardest the Bible teaches. Righteous and intelligent, he couldn't understand why he had suffered so

5. Shelley, *Frankenstein*, 33.
6. *Macbeth* (Bullen), 2.2.62.

much. It embittered him and in his bitterness he repeatedly blamed and questioned God. Finally God decided that he'd had enough so he turned the tables on Job with a single question:

> Where were you when I laid the earth's foundation?
> Tell me, if you understand (Job 38:4 NIV).

Job had no answer.

* * *

Adam's and Eve's rebellion against God didn't just affect how they dealt with the world around them; it affected them personally too. They contaminated their nature with pride when they chose to separate themselves from God. And as the first man and woman, that meant that they also contaminated human nature, their offspring and all of their descendants; Eve after all was so named "because she would become the mother of all the living" (Gen 3:20 NIV). This is what believers mean when they say that Adam and Eve brought sin into the world. This is what we inherited; it's who we are.

Man's lack of knowledge and power meant that he would never "be like God" as he'd desired and as Satan had promised; he struggled and made progress but he ultimately failed to fill the void that God left when he took a step back; and his ignorance and weakness left him vulnerable to what he couldn't foresee and control. He never chose to suffer from natural disasters and diseases or from human error and mistakes, but he did choose to rely on himself instead of God. His pride, ignorance and weakness—our pride, ignorance and weakness—is the root of these forms of suffering.

We can learn from our mistakes so we don't repeat them. We should continue to pursue the knowledge that can alleviate what ails us. It's important that we try to help our fellow man; in fact God commands us to do so. But we should do it in the right spirit, remembering why we're burdened with these afflictions, the magnitude of the void we're trying to fill and what we can and cannot expect to accomplish.

* * *

So God didn't afflict man; he allowed man to afflict himself. Free will, therefore, is the ultimate cause of our suffering whether it be from an intentional act or natural disaster. Or to put it more precisely, our abuse of free will explains all of our suffering. Nonetheless we're left to wonder, Why would a loving God give us free will in the first place?

He gave us free will because it would be impossible for him to give us anything more or better.

Recall that God is perfect, and therefore has no superior; and he's supreme, and therefore has no equal. By definition he can't duplicate himself; he can't create a twin God. Whatever he creates must be imperfect and inferior to him.

If that's the case, what's the next best thing that God can create? It would be something that shares his image and likeness, but isn't a duplicate; it would be something that shares his characteristics, like free will, but wouldn't always make the same choices he would; it would be like him, but imperfect and inferior to him.

It would be . . . us. In an odd way, we're the best he can do.

Nonetheless he's a loving God so we have to ask, Where is God's love amidst our suffering?

To help us answer the question, let's look around us. We can find clues in the unlikeliest places. For example take . . . baseball.

* * *

He was fourteen pounds at birth, the only one of four siblings to survive infancy; his mother Christina said he was the "big egg I have in my basket."[7] His raw physical strength showed itself early. When he was just seventeen years old he played an exhibition in Chicago's Wrigley Field and hit a home run out of the ballpark.

---

7. Reis, *Gehrig*, 8.

Intelligent and shy, he attended Columbia University for two years and majored in engineering before the New York Yankees drafted him. They'd seen how his precise motor skills harnessed prodigious strength, producing seemingly effortless coordination and power. He was an ideal ballplayer in the making.

He served his team well; reporters and fans called him the "Iron Horse" because, from 1925 to 1939, he never took a day off. He played in 2130 consecutive games despite seventeen fractures in his hands and intense back pain later in his career. But none of those injuries would stop him from hitting 493 home runs, winning two Most Valuable Player awards and playing in every All Star game for which he was eligible. And there are other statistics and exploits that, after it was all over, would put Lou Gehrig in baseball's Hall of Fame.

1938 was a good year for him. Still something was missing. He had 170 hits and twenty nine homeruns, both good numbers, but those were his lowest totals in over a decade; and his .295 batting average, good enough to be among the better hitters in the league, was the lowest of his career. At age thirty-five was he just another athlete past his prime? Maybe, but he would later admit that he "tired midseason. I don't know why, but I just couldn't get going again."[8] Of all things, nobody would have expected the Iron Horse to tire.

It got worse. When the following season got underway he was struggling just to run the bases. James Kahn, a reporter for the New York Sun, was worried:

> I think there is something wrong with him. Physically wrong I mean. I don't know what it is, but I am satisfied that it goes far beyond his ball-playing.[9]

His wife, Eleanor, heard the unusual thump as he walked and saw the utensils slip from his hands; his roommate, catcher Bill Dickey, remembered him standing still and looking out of a window in his

---

8. Sontheimer, *Diseases*, 137.
9. Goldstein, "Long Ago Diamond," 13.

SUFFERING

hotel room when suddenly his leg gave out "just as though somebody had tapped him sharply at the back on the knee joint."[10]

The Yankees manager Joe McCarthy saw it all unfold. He was quiet and intelligent man, respectful of players and umpires, more psychologist than drill sergeant. He was like Lou Gehrig in other words, and he saw Gehrig as a father sees a son. As Gehrig's play went from bad to worse McCarthy couldn't bring himself to take the Iron Horse out of the lineup.

But he wasn't the only person who could make the move. On May 2, 1939, in a hotel room in Detroit, McCarthy heard a knock on the door. It was Gehrig. He told McCarthy that he was benching himself "for the good of the team."[11] He'd played in 2130 consecutive games, and he would never play another.

Six weeks later, on his birthday, doctors at the Mayo Clinic told him why. He had amyotrophic lateral sclerosis, an incurable and fatal disease that would slowly destroy his nervous system, first weakening his muscles, then paralyzing them, then making it so he couldn't breathe. It's unclear whether they gave him the prognosis; the custom of the day was to only tell the head of the household and Eleanor had convinced the doctors that she held that role (she'd told them that Lou had given her charge of the couple's finances). She certainly never told him about the prognosis; she was afraid, as she put it, that he might take "that extra pill" so as not to be a burden to her.[12]

After he got the diagnosis he remained hopeful in public and in his letters to his wife but he knew what lay ahead for him; just a few weeks after he visited the Mayo Clinic, a troop of boy scouts greeted him at a train station in Washington, D.C. and wished him luck. Gehrig turned to a sportswriter for the New York Herald Tribune. "They're wishing me luck," he said, "and I'm dying."[13]

For an idea of what people may have known about Gehrig's prognosis, it's telling that major league baseball, the stodgiest of

10. Kaden, "ALS," lines 105–106.
11. Kashatus, *Lou Gehrig*, 128.
12. Krieger, "Eleanor Gehrig," lines 247–248.
13. Kashatus, *Lou Gehrig*, 95.

83

organizations, bent a rule just for him, and it was a big one. The next election for baseball's highest honor, the Hall of Fame, was set for 1942, three years away; but Gehrig was made eligible for induction and was voted into the Hall of Fame just a few months after his retirement in 1939. Although by then he was too depleted to attend the induction ceremony.

His team honored him in a ceremony at Yankee Stadium between games on July 4, 1939. By this time his full diagnosis had been made public. Teammates past and present assembled on the field along with some dignitaries. Dozens of newspaper reporters were there to write about the ceremony, and 61,808 fans filled the stands.

The stadium groundskeepers and janitors gave him gifts. Fiorello LaGuardia spoke to the crowd like the mayor he was, complimenting Gehrig's sportsmanship and citizenship. Joe McCarthy spoke too, a little more personally. He talked about the day when Gehrig told him he was quitting "because you felt yourself a hindrance to the team."[14] McCarthy, struggling to control his emotions, turned to Gehrig and said, "My God, man, you were never that."[15]

Amidst all the accolades he stood with his hat in his hand and with his head bowed as if he was embarrassed by the attention. He wiped away tears, lost in his thoughts as the speeches droned on. It was a sweltering hot day and Joe McCarthy feared that Gehrig would collapse in the heat because he was slowly rocking back and forth as he stood. One newsreel showed Gehrig accepting a trophy from McCarthy; unable to hold it for long, he gingerly put it down on the ground next to other trophies and gifts. A photographer took a picture. The image made for a poignant metaphor; with the trophies at his feet, he stood debilitated and frail but taller than the symbols of his professional accomplishments.

After the speeches ended the public address announcer told the crowd that Gehrig had asked to be excused without making any remarks. They wouldn't let him go; they called for him.

14. Levy, *Joe McCarthy*, 249.
15. Levy, *Joe McCarthy*, 249.

McCarthy whispered some words of encouragement, and the Iron Horse stepped to the microphone.

He started by describing his fatal illness as a "bad break."[16] Then he said something unexpected, something that seemed to make no sense; he said, "today, I consider myself the luckiest man on the face of the earth."[17] He explained how a man in his situation could feel that way. He thanked the Yankees general manager, his teammates and the fans, but also the groundskeepers and ushers. And he paid tribute to his parents and his wife. He was suffering but, somehow, he was also filled with gratitude.

Then he said, "I've got an awful lot to live for."[18]

In the time he had left he became a parole commissioner for $5700 per year. There was nothing glamorous about it and it was the least lucrative offer he'd received in retirement. He wasn't naive about criminals, saying those who endangered the community should remain in prison. But he took the position because he had sympathy for those who'd learned their lesson. "We don't want anyone in jail," he explained, "who can make good."[19]

In his first year on the job, the disease progressed and his strength and coordination deteriorated but he pushed himself to review over 6000 cases, carefully keeping himself out of the newspapers when he visited prisons for interviews. At first Eleanor took notes for him. Eventually the man who once had the strength to hit almost 500 home runs despite seventeen fractures in his hands, couldn't hold a pen; Eleanor had to steady his hand so he could sign official documents. Then, just a little over a year into the job, the Iron Horse quietly resigned when he simply couldn't function anymore. He died on June 2, 1941, sixteen years to the day that he started his first of 2130 consecutive games. He was thirty seven years old.

* * *

16. "Luckiest Man."
17. "Luckiest Man."
18. "Luckiest Man."
19. Robinson, "Hall of Fame," 567.

John Jordan "Buck" O'Neill Jr. was ninety four years old, still sound of wind and limb, and mentally sharp. He was being interviewed by a columnist when he decided to answer a question with a question.

"Son," he said, "what has my life been about?"[20]

If all you knew about Buck O'Neill were some of the things that had happened to him, you would have answered with one word—rejection.

He was born in Carrabelle, Florida in 1911. When he was a young boy his family moved to Sarasota where his father worked in a sawmill and as a foreman at a celery farm, and his mother was a restaurant manager. They worked hard and set an example for him. He carried crates in the fields where he and his father worked under the blistering Florida sun. Buck was unusually strong, carrying four at a time when others managed only two. During lunchtime one day he sat exhausted behind a stack of boxes, "sweating and itching," he recalled, "in that muck":

> I said, "Damn, there's got to be something better than this." I didn't know my father heard me. . . . I thought he was going to reprimand me for saying "damn." . . . Instead, he said, "Son, there is something better. But you have to go out and get it."[21]

Back then like today, major league teams trained for the upcoming season in balmy Florida during February and March. Growing up in Sarasota meant that Buck got to see the New York Yankees. He'd played baseball since he was twelve years old but he'd never seen anything like Babe Ruth, Lou Gehrig and the rest of the players who hit the ball so hard it they were known as "murderers row." When his uncle took him to West Palm Beach to see other professional ball players, he was hooked; he saw the "something better" he hoped he'd find.

And like so many country boys, he left the farm for baseball.

He was good enough to play professionally but he never got an offer to play for the Yankees or any other major league team. So

---

20. Vahe, "Buck O'Neil," 55.
21. Ward, *Baseball*, 226.

he played in other leagues, always looking over his shoulder to see if someone saw what he had to offer. In the prime of his career he was an accomplished player, hitting for the highest average in his league twice. He hoped it would be good enough to get the call but in the eleven years he played, nobody ever noticed.

After retiring as a player he stayed in the game he loved and steadily climbed the ladder of professional baseball. He managed ball clubs that he used to play against and he had tremendous success, winning four championships in eight years. Maybe the Yankees or the Dodgers or the Cubs would be interested in him as a coach or manager in the big leagues?

Nothing.

The fact was, there was something about John Jordan O'Neil Jr. that weighed on him and kept him from the success that should have been his.

The problem wasn't his knowledge of the game or the way he treated people; he had command of baseball's nuances and complexities, and as a coach he mixed a zeal to compete with a genial disposition. If you were on his team he knew you as a person, not just as a player, and he could change the way you played the game because he could change the way you lived your life.

There was a player named Ernie Banks for instance. When he started playing for O'Neil, Banks was a true introvert. "I didn't care for people," Banks said. "I always kind of ran from human beings."[22]

O'Neil knew it was a problem; it impaired Banks' performance on the field because it inhibited his love for the game. "Be alive, man," Buck would yell at him, "you've got to love this game to play it!"[23] Gradually O'Neil changed Banks' outlook, so much so that the introvert who didn't care for people somehow came to believe that "the main thing in my life is making friends."[24] Eventually, he said, "I couldn't wake up fast enough" to get to the ballpark.[25]

22. Martinez, "The Role," lines 12–13.
23. Posnanski, "Remembering Ernie Banks," lines 39–40.
24. NPR, "Remembering Ernie Banks," lines 42–43.
25. NPR, "Wrigley Field," lines 79–80.

With that foundation Banks' talent blossomed and he had a stellar career. He played major league baseball and was "Mr. Cub" to the Chicago fans who loved him and to baseball fans around the country. He had power, swatting over 500 home runs; and he had agility, playing shortstop, the most demanding position on the diamond, at an elite level. He won everyone over, even Manager Leo Durocher, the curmudgeon who groused that "Nice guys finish last." Banks, he said, was "the one nice guy who finished first."[26]

After Banks retired he looked back on his career and O'Neil's influence on him. "I was just so thrilled to have someone like him to show that interest in me," he said, "and I just fell in love with the game of baseball and it was my whole life, and it was because of him."[27]

Still, somehow, Banks' story didn't land Buck a coaching job with the Cubs. But it did open the door to a lesser position; O'Neil accepted an offer to scout prospects for them. He would spend seven hard years on the road, driving into big cities and down dirt roads to scout talent, all while the Cubs promoted one mediocrity after another to manage and lead the team to seven consecutive losing seasons. One of his finds was base stealing legend Lou Brock and more great players followed. Then, finally, in 1962, they made Buck O'Neil an assistant coach. He was fifty one years old.

Even this promotion was bittersweet; no sooner had the Cubs hired him than they announced, "Buck O'Neil will serve in the capacity of an instructor and as such will not be considered a potential head coach or manager."[28] He took the job, though, so he could live his dream of stepping onto a major league baseball field to coach the Chicago Cubs. And even if they hired him with the understanding that he'd never lead the team, he coveted the chance that, somehow, something might happen.

The opportunity came on July 15. With Buck and another coach in the dugout and Charlie Metro managing, the Cubs played the Houston Colt 45's in a doubleheader. In the first

26. Simon, "Remembering Chicago Cub," lines 21–22.
27. Thompson, "The Greatest Ambassador," lines 16–17.
28. Wilson, *Let's Play Two*, 129.

inning of the second game, Charlie Metro argued a call and the umpire ejected him.

Whereupon the coach at third moved to manager, the first base coach moved to third base, and Buck's colleague in the dugout took over at first base.

Then the umpire ejected the second Cubs manager and Buck knew his chance had come to step onto the field and coach. He expected to go to third base, since it was the most demanding base to coach and required the most experience. As the third base coach walked to the dugout to take over as manager, and the first base coach (who had much less experience than Buck) stayed put, Buck stood up and started to walk up the dugout steps to go to third base—when he saw the pitching coach (of all people) coming in from the outfield bullpen to coach third base. He turned around and sat down. Coaching third base was one step away from managing, but the chance disappeared as quickly as it had arisen. That's when he knew, he said, that "there was no chance of that happening."[29]

He never forgot what had happened that day. "After 40 years in baseball and ten as a manager, I was pretty sure I knew when to wave somebody home and when to make him put on the brakes," he said. "I would have gotten a huge thrill out of being on a major league field during a game."[30]

Three men managed the Cubs that year as part of the club's "College of Coaches," a bizarre experiment in which the Cubs rotated coaches to manage the team. They were Charlie Metro, Elvin Tappe and Lou Klein, and they collectively lead the team to 103 losses, a franchise record.

That was strike one.

So O'Neil became a scout again, enduring the travel and daily grind while he searched for prodigies anywhere he might find them. His career could have wound down and ended there but, five years into his second stint as a scout, another opportunity arose. It was even bigger than the chance to manage the team on the field.

29. Wilson, *Let's Play Two*, 129.
30. O'Neil, *Right On Time*, 213–214.

The Cubs general manager had passed away, the owner said he was going to replace him from within, and, suddenly, Buck had a chance to be the general manager of the whole organization—he'd be in charge of field managers and coaches, players and scouts, major league and minor league operations. He was one of just five men interviewed for the job; then he was one of the final two candidates. It looked good. As an experienced scout and a coach:

> I knew every ball player in the Cub organization. . . . I went to spring training with the Cubs; I worked the Cubs ballplayers; when they left I worked the AAA team; when they left I worked the AA team; when they left I worked A. I knew every kid in the Cubs system; I knew every manager; I knew every coach; I knew the general manager; I knew the owner.[31]

He knew the game and the Cubs inside and out.

And he didn't get the job.

Buck had gotten his high school diploma late and had gone to college for only two years. The man who got the job, on the other hand, had his bachelors and masters degrees and was working toward his doctorate. Those qualifications may seem odd for a general manager of a baseball team but Buck understood their importance. "The general manager of a ball club," he explained, "might have breakfast with the mayor, he might have lunch with the governor, dinner with the President of the United States."[32] His two years of college education, he said, "didn't tell on me" until the opportunity to be the general manager of the Chicago Cubs came and went.[33]

His lack of a formal education hurt him. He would always wonder "what I might have been had I been able to attend Sarasota High School or matriculated at the University of Florida."[34] He had every other qualification for the job; "I had the baseball," he later

---

31. visionaryproject, "My Baseball Career."
32. visionaryproject, "My Baseball Career."
33. visionaryproject, "My Baseball Career."
34. visionaryproject, "My Baseball Career."

said, but "had I had that piece of paper . . .".[35] It cost him the chance of a lifetime, one that he knew would never come again.

It wasn't his fault. He wasn't "able" to go to Sarasota High School because he was black (there were only four high schools in the entire state of Florida that admitted blacks); and he wasn't "able" to matriculate at the University of Florida because he was black. He'd made enough money as a professional ball player to pay for college but his only option was Edward Waters College in Jacksonville, where he had to take some college courses plus the classes that he needed to get his high school diploma. Then he went play baseball in the Negro Leagues, carrying those modest academic credentials with him to support a career after his playing days were over.

Those credentials weren't enough to be a general manager for the Cubs, however, the job for which he was qualified but could only dream about because he didn't have "that piece of paper." And so the consequences of segregation bore down on Buck O'Neil years after Jim Crow disappeared.

Strike two.

As an African American ball player in the thirties, forties and fifties, he'd seen it all. He'd played ball with and against legendary Negro League ballplayers, men like Satchel Page, who he thought was the greatest pitcher ever, and Josh Gibson, who hit the ball so hard it made a sound unlike any other (save, Buck said, when Babe Ruth was at bat).

He'd played against Major League legends, too, when they went "barnstorming" for exhibition games to make some extra money, men like Ruth and Bob Feller and Ted Williams.

He'd played with a minor league team called the "Zulus," whose owner made the players wear grass skirts.

He'd played with the Kansas City Monarchs (who would become Negro League champions). He was on their team when they were scheduled to play a game in Macon, Georgia, until the Ku Klux Klan met them in the dugout. And he was on the road with them in Virginia when their bus stopped for gas and one of his

35. visionaryproject, "My Baseball Career."

teammates went to use the "whites only" restroom. The gas station owner yelled "Hey, boy!" and told him to stop, so he turned around and told the owner that his team would keep its money. When he went to take the hoses out of the bus's two fifty gallon tanks, the owner had second thoughts; he said he could leave the hoses in the tanks. And Jackie Robinson got to use the restroom.

After Buck retired as a player, bigotry would keep him from being a manager for the Cubs and the legacy of segregation would keep him from being their general manager; but he remained a champion for the game of baseball. He wrote an autobiography, "Right On Time," the title and the story refuting the idea that he should have been born later to play the game at the highest level in the Major Leagues; the Negro Leagues, he said, were every bit as good. And he founded the Negro League Baseball Museum, which he dedicated to saving the history of African American baseball from the anonymity to which it and its legends were headed. Why he did it is best summed up by a story he loved to tell about Satchel Paige and Babe Ruth:

> This was in Chicago, after Ruth came out of the major leagues. He was barnstorming, playing with different teams, and he played us. Satchel was pitching and Ruth was hitting . . . Ruth hit the ball, must have been 500 feet, off of Satchel. Satchel looked at Ruth all the way around the bases and when Ruth got to home plate, you know who shook his hand? Satchel Paige shook Ruth's hand at home plate. They stopped the game and waited, he and Satchel talking, until the kid went out, got the ball, brought it back, and Satchel had Babe Ruth autograph that ball for him. That was some kind of moment.[36]

Baseball, O'Neil said, was like a religion for him. It had rules and it humbled you; it filled you with hope and it brought people together. And so he created the Negro League Baseball Museum out of love, not bitterness; he celebrated what the African American baseball player had accomplished and he shared it with everyone else. His pupil on the field and in life, Ernie Banks, was famous for

---

36. Ward, *Baseball*, 231.

SUFFERING

saying, "It's a beautiful day, let's play two." That's what the game meant to Banks, he later said, and "that was Buck O'Neil."[37]

* * *

Baseball doesn't just bestow its ultimate honor on those who played the game. It also commemorates its pioneers—owners, executives and umpires, and even quirky contributors to the game like Henry Chadwick, the man who invented the box score. But, players or not, they have one thing in common; they all made the game the marvel that it is.

As an old man John Jordan "Buck" O'Neil's name was placed on the ballot for election to Hall of Fame for just that reason. He spent a lifetime in the game and now, at age ninety four, he stood on the doorsteps to baseball's highest honor. It was a long way from the celery fields of Florida.

And on that day in 2006, when all of the votes were counted, Buck O'Neil fell one vote short.

It could have been strike three but O'Neil, in the midst of this latest rejection, still wasn't thinking about himself. It was the year when seventeen men from the Negro Leagues were voted into the Hall of Fame but all of them were dead. So when he heard the news that he didn't have the votes, he simply dismissed it by saying "that's the way the cookie crumbles."[38] And instead of grousing about it, he wondered if he'd be asked to speak for the men who did have the votes but couldn't speak for themselves. A columnist asked him how he could bring himself to speak for others when the Hall of Fame had just rejected him. And that's when he answered his question with the question, "Son, what has my life been about?"

Of course they asked, and he spoke.

He started by saying that it was "quite an honor" to speak for the players who "helped build a bridge across the chasm of prejudice."[39]

---

37. Posnanski, "Buck," line 90.
38. Vahe, "Buck O'Neil," 48.
39. National Baseball Hall of Fame, "Induction Ceremony Speech."

Then he expanded the scope of his speech by talking about African Americans who owned and operated successful businesses in spite of segregation; there was the Negro Leagues of course, but did you know that it was eclipsed by the entrepreneur Madame C.J. Walker, who made a fortune manufacturing and marketing beauty products for African American women? And insurance companies run by and for African Americans were bigger still.

Then he went in a surprising direction; he left baseball and business behind to send a different message, just like Gehrig had done. He said that despite everything that he and his people had endured, he "never learned to hate. I can't hate a human being," he explained, "because my God never made anything ugly. Now you can be ugly if you want to boy, but God didn't make you that way."[40] Then:

> Martin [Luther King] said agape is understanding, creative, a redemptive good will toward all men. Agape is an overflowing love which seeks nothing in return. And when you reach love on this level you love all men, not because you like them, not because their ways appeal to you, but you love them because God loved them. I love Jehovah my God with all my heart, with all my soul, and I love everyone of you as I love myself.[41]

Here O'Neil was making the same point that Oxford don and renowned theologian C.S. Lewis once made. If love is merely a feeling of affection then it's impossible to love all mankind, much less your enemy. But Lewis discovered something strange about love; he always loved himself, and he always wanted what's right and good for himself, even when he didn't particularly like himself. And since he should love others as himself, he must love others even if, as Buck tenderly put it, their ways don't "appeal to you."

He closed by asking everyone "to do something for me. I want you to hold hands."[42] And when they did he led them through the second verse of a hymn, and everyone on that sultry

40. National Baseball Hall of Fame, "Induction Ceremony Speech."
41. National Baseball Hall of Fame, "Induction Ceremony Speech."
42. National Baseball Hall of Fame, "Induction Ceremony Speech."

summer afternoon slowly sang "the greatest thing . . . in all my life . . . is loving you."[43]

He thanked them, they stood and applauded, and he thanked them again.

The Hall of Fame told Buck O'Neil that there was no room at the inn for him, so he gracefully paid tribute to the contributions and legacies of others. He did so bearing a fresh wound that, at age ninety four, was especially painful; this final rejection came at the end of a long road. But, imitating his Savior, he never stopped loving people through the pain.

Son, what has my life been about?

He didn't know it at the time but he was also dying of cancer. Ken Burns had profiled him in his documentary *Baseball* and he saw O'Neil after the ceremony. "He wasn't the same when he got home from Cooperstown," Burns said. "It was as if his tents were folded."[44] Whatever he felt about the Hall of Fame, he'd given baseball all he had, and so much more than he got. And he was spent.

A few months later Buck O'Neil died, secure in his faith that he'd find something better than what the celery fields, and the Hall of Fame, had to offer.

* * *

"Kennedy Assassinated"
"Man Walks On Moon"

Sometimes the headline says it all. The best of them are concise and jarring statements of significant facts. You recognize the large letters and bold type years later; you remember them.

They're not always serious, however; sometimes the writers have a little fun with their subject. When Dizzy Dean was running the bases and got hit in the head by the second baseman's throw, headlines across the country shared Dean's rendition of his doctors' diagnosis: "They X-Rayed My Head, And Found Nothing."

---

43. National Baseball Hall of Fame, "Induction Ceremony Speech."
44. Huisking, "Changed My Life," 17.

And on rare occasions a headline can be imbued with deep meaning.

There was one such headline in 2010, the year Armando Galarraga, a pitcher for the Detroit Tigers, stood on the brink of perfection.

In the 149 year, 215,000 game history of professional baseball, only twenty three pitchers have thrown a "perfect" game—a game that they pitched, start to finish, without a single batter reaching base from a hit, walk or fielding error. In a nine inning game that means twenty seven batters come up to the plate and twenty seven batters return to the dugout, every one of them beaten by the pitcher.

On June 2, 2010 nobody would have marked Armando Galarraga for perfection. In ten years of professional baseball he'd played for eleven minor league teams and two major league teams. Hampered by surgeries on his elbow and shoulder, he'd compiled a record of fifty one wins against fifty five losses. Yet on that day in Detroit when he was the starting pitcher for the Tigers, he somehow retired the first twenty six Cleveland Indians he'd faced. With his team winning 3-0, only Jason Donald, the twenty seventh batter, stood between him and perfection.

Donald hit a routine ground ball to first baseman Miguel Cabrera, who moved to his right away from first base and fielded it cleanly. Galarraga sprinted to first, caught Cabrera's easy toss and touched the base, beating Donald to the bag by a full step.

And that's when umpire Jim Joyce, one of major league baseball's best, called Donald safe.

It went into the scorebook as a base hit, ruining Galarraga's perfect game.

It took a while for the anger and ugliness to erupt. In the first few moments after the call both Cabrera and Donald simply put their hands on their heads, wide eyed, stunned; Galarraga just looked at Joyce and smiled.

Then Tigers manager Jim Leyland came out of the dugout and, like the Detroit fans in the stands, he gave Joyce an earful.

After their heated argument ended Galarraga took the ball, got the next man out and the game ended.

After it was all over Joyce, who grew up in nearby Toledo, Ohio, drove to see his elderly mother. She was living alone in his boyhood home, Joyce's father having passed earlier in the year. Radio and television played and replayed his blown call, spinning the public's anger into a frenzy; there were death threats, enough so that major league baseball provided security for both Joyce and his mother.

Another story emerged overnight, however. It turned out that after the game had ended, Joyce saw the replay of his call and did something umpires almost never do; he called the media into the umpires' room. He was clearly upset over what he'd done. In front of everyone he admitted that he'd blown the call. And he apologized.

Eventually the media picked up that story. It wasn't highlighted the way the blown call was but it somehow found its way through the noise and hate to anyone who had an ear to hear it. And that set the stage for the next day when the Indians played the Tigers again, and for the headline.

Before every baseball game the umpires gather at home plate to be greeted by each team's coach or manager, who hands the home plate umpire a card with his team's official lineup. It's always a perfunctory scene with handshakes all around, the routine occasionally being broken by a wisecrack or two. On this day, however, it was Jim Joyce's turn to umpire home plate and it would be anything but routine.

The Tigers fans saw him as he walked onto the field but there were no catcalls; instead of laying into him again, making things even more painful, there was a smattering of applause. It slowly spread and got louder until Joyce's emotions started to get the better of him. Then he saw one of the Tigers walking toward him with the team's lineup card; it was Galarraga. He gave it to Joyce and shook his hand, smiling just as he had the night before.

Joyce had been raised in the Midwest and, as a young man, he'd worked on the floor of a factory that built Jeeps; he was tough, modest, not prone to emotional outbursts, but now he was wiping tears from his eyes.

Sports Illustrated told the story beautifully. Joyce reflected on what he'd done to Galarraga, regretting that "I took something away from him."[45] Galarraga remembered how he felt after Joyce's blunder, saying that "I didn't feel bad for me. I felt bad for him."[46] Each man had a reason to dwell on how the call affected him; neither one did.

Someone from the magazine wrote the headline. It encapsulated everything that had happened and how the story transcended baseball; and it said it all in five words. It was "A Different Kind Of Perfect."

* * *

A different kind of perfect . . . It also describes a young man, filled with gratitude and working for others when he knew he was dying; he said he was "the luckiest man on the face of the earth." And it describes an old man, too, one who suffered from decades of bigotry but who responded with love; he answered baseball's final rejection with a hymn, singing "The greatest thing, in all my life, is loving you . . . ."

And it reminds you of Another whose suffering Galarraga, Joyce, Gehrig and O'Neil approximated. He was scourged by the rulers of an empire and crucified at a young age, and he too responded with love.

It's hard to remember the statistics that reflect a ballplayer's accomplishments on the field, even for fans of the game. But if you listen to Gehrig's speech at Yankee Stadium or O'Neil's at Cooperstown, or if you watch the scene at home plate with Galarraga and Joyce, you'll have a hard time forgetting them. Our memories remind us of what's important and what we remember about these men is telling. Is it possible that when we're about our business and in the moment, our notions of perfection

---

45. Verducci, "Different Kind of Perfect," 21.
46. Verducci, "Different Kind of Perfect," 22.

and power are upside down, that we're missing what constitutes life and spins the globe?

God created the first human in his image, but that being was solitary and lonely. So God removed a rib and separated the sexes, creating Adam and Eve. He created us, in other words, to love each other; it's our true nature to do so.

In spite of our Creator's intention that we love one another, Adam and Eve made a bad bargain, one that corrupted our nature and has left us in a terrible predicament where we're bound to suffer. When we do we often respond by lashing out at the world or setting ourselves apart from others; we yield to our corrupted nature, see everyone and everything as hopeless and hostile, and either go to battle or run for cover. Instead we should draw inspiration from his example, face the world and, as Abraham Lincoln's father put it, "hug it the tighter."

Jesus preached that we should fulfill our nature not just by loving our neighbors and friends, but by loving our enemies and praying for those who persecute us; in this way he calls us to "be perfect . . . as your heavenly Father is perfect" (Matt 5:48 NIV). And so we see that being perfect isn't playing the most consecutive games; it isn't being inducted into the Hall of Fame; it isn't retiring the twenty seventh batter or making the right call. When Gehrig, O'Neil, Galarraga and Joyce strove to perfect their true nature, they were doing something else entirely, something even more difficult.

They bore their suffering with dignity.

Each of these men knew what suffering was; they didn't welcome it but when it visited them, they knew that they had to bear it; they knew that battling it would have been in vain because their adversity had become an affliction to be endured, not an obstacle to be overcome. So they accepted it and dispensed with their pride instead, letting it go with what they'd coveted for themselves but lost. And indeed Joyce had suffered a hit to his professional reputation and there was no pride in his apology; Galarraga had lost his place in the record books and there was no pride in his smile and handshake; and O'Neil had lost his place in the Hall of Fame and Gehrig had lost his strength, and there was no pride in their speeches.

There's more to suffering, however, than just the opportunity that it presents for you to do away with your pride. As the pride in your heart shrinks, something else happens, and it happens quite naturally; it leaves a void and the space for God expands. Your humility gives him more room with which to work, and more avenues for him to inspire you. And if you continue to leave your pride behind and allow him to work on you, he'll transform you through and through until you become a stranger to yourself.

Think of the man once known as The Iron Horse, now barely able to hold a pen but using the strength that he had left to sign a recommendation for parole; think of the pitcher who was paid to compete, smiling and shaking the hand of the man who spoiled his historic achievement, and moving the thick skinned umpire to tears with his gesture of forgiveness; and think of the ninety four year old man who wanted to be recognized by the game to which he'd devoted his life, taking the stage right after the Hall of Fame rejected him to talk a little about baseball, and a lot about love.

A legendary player, a journeyman pitcher, a respected umpire and an ambassador of the sport—through their suffering and humility, and with God's love, they all became strangers to their old selves, inspirations to others and, each in his own way, a different kind of perfect.

VI

Gifts

Gold, Frankincense and Myrrh

"Something we were withholding made us weak."[1]
—The Gift Outright (Robert Frost)

Della and her husband were desperately poor. It was the early 1900s and Jim was just getting started in his career. They'd struggled enough when he was making only thirty dollars a week; now all he brought home was twenty dollars a week.

It was Christmas Eve. For months Della had saved every nickel she could to buy Jim a present, but all she could save was one dollar and eighty seven cents. She was awfully upset about it; she thought she'd never find the right gift.

This is the beginning of O. Henry's *The Gift of the Magi*, a short story consistently ranked among the best in the history of American literature. It's been translated into dozens of languages and adapted in foreign films. American television shows, from comedies like *The Honeymooners* to children's programs like *Sesame Street*, have amused their audiences with their versions of it. And it's continued to pop up in the unlikeliest places; Pankaj

---

1. Frost, "The Gift," 907.

Udhas, a singer from India, recorded a song with a music video that features the young couple from the fable.

Written in 1906, *The Gift of the Magi* is just six pages long. But that's all O. Henry needed to tell the story about how Della somehow managed to buy her husband an invaluable gift, and how Jim did the same for her. Its irony and plot twist explain some of its popularity, but they don't explain its broad, almost universal appeal. The reason why so many artists from all over the world have adapted it for over a century, right down to an Indian singer and his music video, is because it says something fundamental about human nature.

There's a lot in it, more than you think when you read the story for the first time. The basic plot is simple and compact. As O. Henry tells it, Della cuts her long and exceptionally beautiful hair and sells it so she can afford to buy Jim a gold chain for his pocket watch, one that he treasures because his father and grandfather had worn it. Unfortunately, at the same time, Jim sells his pocket watch to buy Della jeweled combs for her beautiful hair. So when they give each other their gifts on Christmas Eve, the gifts themselves are useless.

Of course when Della's hair grows back, and if Jim finds a way to make enough money so he can buy another pocket watch, their gifts will be useful to them. But at the moment when they exchanged them, the jeweled combs and the gold chain had no practical value. They did signify the love between Jim and Della, however, and that's one of the lessons of the fable. A wonderful gift usually points to something else that makes it special; what a gift represents is often more important than the gift itself.

Della's and Jim's gifts represented a couple of things in particular. One of them was sacrifice; each parted with a treasured possession to give the other a thoughtful gift. Their sacrifice gave value to the objects that they gave each other, and like any genuine sacrifice, theirs wasn't easy. When Della decided to cut her hair, she felt the way we all feel when we give up something we love for the sake of someone we love more. O. Henry wrote that Della's "eyes were shining brilliantly" as she thought about what she had to do, "but her face had lost its color."[2] Then he summed up her love for Jim in a sobering way. "Love and large hearted giving, when added together, can leave deep marks."[3]

It's like the story of the widow's mite from the gospels of Mark and Luke. After wealthy people fill the coffers of the temple's treasury, a poor widow contributes the equivalent of a few pennies. Jesus watches it all and says that she gave more than the others. The rich gave "gave their gifts out of their wealth," he says, "but she out of her poverty put in all she had to live on" (Luke 21:4 NIV).

Della's gift represented something else, too. The gold chain was "plain and simple" but for some reason "as soon as she saw it, she knew that Jim must have it."[4] Why did she feel compelled to buy something that seemed so ordinary? It made her think; in an instant she knew why. "Quietness and value," she realized, "Jim and the chain both had quietness and value."[5] The gift brought to the surface and represented his best qualities, making them manifest and tangible. It reminded her of why she loved him. And maybe the gold chain would also remind Jim of why she loved him, and inspire him to continue to make quietness and value as manifest in his character as they were in her gift.

Likewise for Christian believers, the magi's gifts of gold, frankincense and myrrh represented the divinity of Jesus. Gold represented his power and authority; frankincense, his holiness; and myrrh (paradoxically), his death. The kings from the east gave them to Jesus when he was an infant; the gifts themselves couldn't possibly have been of any use to him. Instead, they represented who he was.

Putting aside O. Henry's classic for a moment and looking at our own lives, we see how the occasions on which we give gifts also say a lot about us. We almost always give them to commemorate a fresh start or new beginning. We give them on birthdays, Christmas and Hanukkah; at confirmations and bar mitzvahs; at

---

2. Henry, *Selected Stories*, 26.
3. Henry, "The Gift," 4.
4. Henry, "The Gift," 3.
5. Henry, "The Gift," 3.

weddings and on anniversaries; to a patient leaving the hospital or a soldier returning from war; for a housewarming or to someone who's leaving to go to college or starting a new job. All of these occasions have something in common; they mark a threshold that we're crossing on our way to some sort of renewal, one that can be a cause for both celebration and trepidation; venturing into the unknown tends to have that effect on us.

And, of course, before we give a gift, we wrap (or hide) it. We conceal it just to surprise the recipient. It's a familiar routine that we reprise for every occasion but it never gets stale. Giving a thoughtful gift is like setting a table; we may do it the same way every day, but that doesn't mean the meal isn't delicious.

It's an interesting custom because we follow it all of the time without really knowing why. When you think about what makes for a heartfelt and thoughtful gift, however, you have your answer. We box and wrap a gift because concealing it represents what's missing in our daily lives. A gift is supposed to surface someone's good qualities that may be buried and dormant, or that we don't notice and appreciate like we should; and our willingness to sacrifice something for someone else's sake, and the occasions for celebrating a renewal, seem so rare. So we conceal the gift to represent their absence. And when the gift is opened . . . surprise!

This is why giving gifts can be stressful. Giving a thoughtful gift means sacrificing something you want for someone's else's sake; thinking about his good qualities and finding a gift that reflects them; wrapping (or hiding) the gift until the occasion finally arrives; and then presenting the gift in the spirit of renewal that the occasion celebrates. And even when we don't check all of those boxes, we intuitively feel that we should. Giving a meaningful gift is hard to do.

Nonetheless, we put ourselves through this stress year after year, sometimes to the point of souring the occasion that the gift is supposed to commemorate. It begs the question, Why do we follow this custom so painstakingly?

Our hypothesis is, the gift of Jesus Christ. "For God so loved the world," reads John 3:16, "that he *gave* his only begotten Son

...." His life, death and resurrection are the inspiration for our thoughtful and heartfelt gifts.

* * *

If you think of Jesus as a gift, you don't have to look far to find the sacrifice that he made by giving himself to us. The story of his Passion leading up to his crucifixion is familiar to all Christians. On the night before he was crucified, Jesus sweated blood in the Garden of Gethsemane; the next day he wore a crown of thorns, was beaten and mocked and made to carry a heavy cross 2000 feet along the Via Dolorosa, the Way of Suffering, only to be crucified on the cross that he bore. His sacrifice was real; his pain was real. When he was crucified, he was in agony from his many wounds. He bled from the nails in his hands and legs; he suffocated and died on a cross.

Love and large hearted giving, when added together, can leave deep marks.

Jesus never denied his divinity but it was concealed in many ways throughout his life. He was born in a manger in a small and unimportant town; he was a mere carpenter by profession; he rode a donkey into Jerusalem to face his accusers; and, of course, he was crucified and laid to rest in a tomb that was sealed. And three days later when the boulder that sealed the tomb was removed, the Gift within it . . . was missing.

Surprise!

The empty tomb proved that a threshold had been crossed, marking a renewal unlike any other. The women who saw the empty tomb knew what sort of renewal it was; inspired by his example, they knew that they too must make gifts of themselves as he did. And, knowing what he'd endured, it filled them with conflicting emotions; the Bible says the sight of the empty tomb left them "afraid yet filled with joy" (Matthew 28:8 NIV).

Della's *"eyes were shining brilliantly but her face had lost its color."*

So Jesus checks the first three boxes for a thoughtful and heartfelt gift. He sacrifices himself for us; he is a surprise to us; and he marks an occasion of renewal. All that's left is the good within us that he makes manifest and tangible.

What is the good that the gift of Jesus represents? Our names for him tell us. We call him our redeemer and savior; teacher and master; mediator and advocate; our shepherd and the way, the truth and the life; and the lamb of God and bread of life. Add it all up and what God gives us in the person of Jesus is the greatest gift of all, that of pure love, totally selfless and ultimately sacrificial.

There's an issue, however. Unlike the gold chain that represented Jim's "quietness and value," the gift of Jesus doesn't represent what's within us; ever since Adam rebelled against God, we've been tainted by sin and are incapable of *agape*, the perfect love of God. We don't have what he makes manifest and tangible. In that sense then, he's not like the gift in O. Henry's story.

But there's one more thing about gifts that explains how the ability to love like him can arise within us. And this time it has nothing to do with how we give a gift; it's about accepting what he's offered us and reciprocating in kind.

* * *

In *All I Really Need To Know I Learned In Kindergarten*, Robert Fulghum tells a story about a stranger that he met at the airport in Bombay, India, many years ago:

> I had come to reclaim my bags and had no Indian currency left. The agent would not take a traveler's check, and I was uncertain about getting my luggage and making my plane. The man paid my claim check fee—about eighty cents—and told me [a] story as a way of refusing my attempt to figure out how to repay him.[6]

The man told Fulghum about an Indian civil servant, someone named Menon, who once was destitute and needed a small sum

---

6. Fulghum, *All I Really Need*, 126.

of money to tide him over. Menon ran into a Sikh, who gave him fifteen rupees on the condition that he repay the debt by giving the same sum of money "to any stranger who came to him in need, as long as he lived."[7] The Sikh told him that "the help came from a stranger and was to be repaid to a stranger."[8]

Menon had an assistant who heard the story, and he passed it on to his son—who was the man Fulghum met at the airport. And that man . . .

> . . . had continued the tradition of seeing himself in debt to strangers, whenever, however.
>
> From a nameless Sikh to an Indian civil servant to his assistant to his son to me, a white foreigner in a moment of frustrating inconvenience. The gift was not large as money goes, and my need was not great, but the spirit of the gift is beyond price and leaves me blessed and in debt.[9]

What the story says is what we've all felt; when someone gives us a gift, he leaves us feeling blessed and in debt.

Notice too how, in a sense, the type of debt we owe usually corresponds to the type of gift we receive. We tend to repay what we've been given; we reciprocate in kind. A stranger gives you fifteen rupees; you give fifteen rupees to a stranger.

Apply that rule to the story about the Sikh, and it will lead you to an unexpected place. The Sikh told Menon, not just to give fifteen rupees to a stranger to satisfy his debt; he told him to give fifteen rupees to everyone that he meets who's in need for the rest of his life. And the stranger that Fulghum met in the airport believed he was "in debt to strangers, whenever, however." Repaying the gift of the Sikh was clearly different than, say, repaying a bank loan. For one thing, the Sikh didn't want the money back; and unlike a bank, he forgave the debt but multiplied the obligation to everyone else.

---

7. Fulghum, *All I Really Need*, 126.
8. Fulghum, *All I Really Need*, 126.
9. Fulghum, *All I Really Need*, 126–127.

What the Sikh gave Menon was something that no bank could give. He didn't just give Menon fifteen rupees; *he created a spirit of charity in Menon.* It was a gift beyond price and it changed him; he carried it with him for the rest of his life. And like any spiritual gift, it grew within him and spread beyond him.

The parallel is clear. Jesus loved us selflessly and sacrificed his life for us, so he too left us blessed and in debt. *He creates a spirit of agape in us*, which is a gift beyond price; it changes us. We should carry it with us the rest of our lives so it, like any spiritual gift, can grow within us and spread beyond us.

In a word, he inspires us. We should stop and think about what it means to inspire someone. It's not just a pat on the back or an encouraging word; the Oxford English dictionary says that to inspire means "to *fill* someone, or *create* in someone, the *urge or ability to do or feel something*, especially something *creative*." When God gave his only begotten son, he was a creator once again, breathing his spirit of love into man. And we are born again.

"We love," John says in his first letter, "because he first loved us" (1 John 4:19 NIV).

He checks the final box; he is the gift that represents the pure love within us because he creates it within us. Like the gold chain and the jeweled combs, he too is a gift beyond price.

We must always remember that only he can create in us the desire and ability to love in this way; it isn't a gift that a sinful man can give, because a sinful man doesn't have it to give. God, and God alone, makes it possible for us to have a fresh start and a new beginning, reversing the course of our nature so that we may become, not merely good or better (". . . that has no relish of salvation in't . . ."),[10] but "perfect, as your heavenly Father is perfect" (Matt 5:48 NIV).

* * *

All that said, following up on the inspiration and repaying the debt doesn't happen automatically as if it were a product of a simple

---

10. Hamlet (Bullen), 3.3.90.

formula or mechanical process. When God offers his spirit of love, you have a choice; you can take it in or you can turn away, rejecting the offer or ignoring it as if it was never made. It's a critically important point; if you want to love like he did, then you must open your heart and mind to him. "After all," wrote C.S. Lewis, "you must have a capacity to receive, or even omnipotence can't give."[11]

Robert Frost's poem *The Gift Outright* tells us why we might turn away from God, at least at first. The poem is about the American continent, which was a gift to the settlers who came to the new world from England. They failed to recognize it for what it was, however, because, at first sight, it was just a harsh and untamed wilderness— "unstoried, artless, unenhanced".[12] They thought the land would make them miserable; it intimidated them. "[W]e were England's, still colonials," Frost wrote.[13] At that time . . .

> Something we were withholding made us weak.
>
> We found out that it was ourselves
>
> We were withholding from our land of living . . .[14]

God offers us something greater than a new frontier and yet, just like the colonials in Frost's poem, many of us are withholding ourselves from him.

Why? Remember the women's emotional reaction to the empty tomb; they felt great joy but they were also afraid. It's our fear that keeps us from accepting what Jesus offers.

The fear is only natural; it's part of the package. If you accept the blessing, then you incur a debt; you have to reciprocate in kind. Accepting *agape* means practicing *agape*, and that can be frightening. Of course rejecting it has consequences too, and they may prove to be catastrophic. It's a tough choice to have to make but that's how God intended it.

---

11. Lewis, *Signature Classics*, 676.
12. Frost, "The Gift," 907.
13. Frost, "The Gift," 907.
14. Frost, "The Gift," 907.

Shakespeare's *The Twelfth Night*, a romantic comedy of sorts, includes a famous passage that's usually quoted out of context but is still worth reading for the encouragement it gives us when we're facing a pivotal choice:

> Be not afraid of greatness. Some are born great, some achieve greatness, and some have greatness thrust upon 'em. Thy fates open their hands. Let thy blood and spirit embrace them.[15]

With apologies to the greatest writer in the English language, let's adapt it for our own purposes, substituting a cross for greatness to convey how Jesus' gift has left us blessed and in debt, and how we should embrace it:

> Be not afraid of the cross. Some are born on a cross, some take up a cross, some have a cross thrust upon them. God has opened his hands. Let thy blood and spirit embrace him.

Rest assured this debt comes with a promise unlike any other, that your fear will yield to everlasting joy.

* * *

Accept the blessing. At first the colonials in Frost's poem hugged the coastline that connected them to England, turning their backs on the wilderness that stretched westward. Eventually they came to accept the land for the blessing that it was; slowly the spirit of the pioneer grew within them.

Similarly, face Jesus and allow him to breathe his spirit of love into you. He isn't going anywhere; he's waiting for you to turn. Let the spirit of *agape* grow within you.

Pay the debt. As the spirit of the pioneer grew within them, the colonials repaid their debt by taming the wilderness, cultivating the land and building towns. Their blood and spirit embraced the land that once intimidated them; they went west.

---

15. Twelfth Night (Bullen), 2.5.142–145.

As the spirit of *agape* grows within you, repay your debt by loving his creation and all mankind, and by sacrificing yourself, even your life, for everyone that you meet in need. Let your blood and spirit embrace him; let the spirit of *agape* spread beyond you.

It will change you. The blessing and the debt changed the colonials forever. As they built cities and towns and founded churches and schools, they changed the landscape and it changed them; they became pioneers and settlers, merchants and farmers. They no longer belonged to a king; as Frost wrote, they "gave themselves outright" to the land and "forthwith found salvation in surrender."[16] They became Americans.

If you accept the life, death and resurrection of Jesus as a blessing and pay the debt by practicing *agape*, it will change you forever; when you give yourself outright to Jesus, you become a child of God.

Jesus gave his life for you, and you can give it back again. This is how you atone; this is how you will be reconciled to him. "For whoever wants to save their life will lose it," he said, "but whoever loses their life for me will find it" (Matt 16:25 NIV).

Let him live within you so you can reciprocate and atone as he did. It may seem hard at first but it's nowhere near impossible; in fact, if you've ever received a gift with gratitude and felt inspired to give one in return, you may have already welcomed him without even knowing it.

---

16. Frost, "The Gift," 907.

VII

Sabbath

Remember the Sabbath day,
to keep it holy

"Then He said to them, The Sabbath was made for man, not man for the Sabbath."

Mr. Darcy was a wealthy man who was surrounded by beautiful women but he never fell in love with any of them. Elizabeth Bennett knew why even if he didn't know or care. Being a lively and playful sort, she told him:

> The fact is, that you were sick of civility, of deference, of officious attention. You were disgusted with the women who were always speaking, and looking, and thinking, for your approbation alone. . . . [I]n your heart, you thoroughly despised the persons who so assiduously courted you.[1]

Mr. Darcy was used to that type of attention. The women he met acted like they loved him because he was their ticket to a secure and comfortable life at Pemberley House, his large estate in the country. They looked right past him to the mansion, grounds and gardens.

---

1. Austen, *Pride and Prejudice*, 392.

Elizabeth and Mr. Darcy eventually fall in love in *Pride and Prejudice*, the classic by Jane Austen. It's all about the relationship between those unlikely lovers and it's an entertaining story. But even though it focuses on romantic love, it isn't overly sentimental and its lead characters don't drown in their feelings. It exposes the complexities of love and the practical problems lovers face. And it also tells us a few things about our relationship with God.

Jesus told us to "love the Lord your God with all your heart and with all your soul and with all your mind" (Matt 22:37 NIV). Picking up on what Elizabeth said in *Pride and Prejudice* we should ask ourselves, Do we love our Savior, or do we love salvation? There's a difference; as Elizabeth pointed out, pretending to love Mr. Darcy while actually loving Pemberley House means you're a sycophant and a flatterer, not a companion. Do we pretend to love Jesus just because he's our ticket to heaven? If so we need to forget the reward for loving him, quit looking past him and, instead, simply focus on him.

There's another aspect to Elizabeth's and Mr. Darcy's relationship that will help us understand what to expect when we focus on God; it wasn't love at first sight. When Elizabeth asked Mr. Darcy why he fell in love with her, he told her it was a long time ago so he couldn't "fix on the hour, or the spot, or the look, or the words, which laid the foundation."[2] But he did remember one thing; he fell in love without knowing it. "I was in the middle," he told her, "before I knew that I had begun."[3]

Elizabeth had the same experience. She told her sister that her love for Mr. Darcy "has been coming on so gradually that I hardly know when it began."[4]

They may not have been aware of their love for each other because they didn't mix well, at least at first. She sparred with him and he parried in return. There's a telling scene early in the story that shows how each of them contributed to the friction; Mr. Darcy wouldn't dance with Elizabeth at a ball because she was

---

2. Austen, *Pride and Prejudice*, 392.
3. Austen, *Pride and Prejudice*, 392.
4. Austen, *Pride and Prejudice*, 385.

beneath his social class, and she hastily concluded that his bad manners revealed his true character. In other words the problem was his pride and her prejudice.

There was also some tension between Elizabeth and Mr. Darcy but unlike the friction from their pride and prejudice, the tension was healthy. It came from the recognition that they each lacked the virtues that the other possessed. Elizabeth, as usual, saw it first:

> She began now to comprehend that he was exactly the man who, in disposition and talents, would most suit her.... It was a union that must have been to the advantage of both; by her ease and liveliness, his mind might have been softened, his manners improved; and from his judgment, information and knowledge of the world, she must have received benefit of greater importance.[5]

When Elizabeth recognized Mr. Darcy's virtues she came to see her own shortcomings, and that she needed him and would become dependent upon him. And the same was true for Mr. Darcy. At first it made them a little wary of growing closer but eventually it created a bond between them.

So despite the friction borne of pride and prejudice and wariness of becoming dependent upon one another, their love grew because there was chemistry between them; they were better together. Their love wasn't smothered by perpetual romance and infatuation; it was often tense but it was a creative and dynamic tension.

There may be tension in your relationship with God, too; like the relationship between Elizabeth and Mr. Darcy you may be reluctant to get closer to him because his holiness can make you uncomfortable; it reveals what you lack. He's someone you'll need, someone you'll have to depend on. But that's okay; the tension is a sign of chemistry.

Make that chemistry work in your relationship with God. Don't look past him to the reward that he promises; focus

---

5. Austen, *Pride and Prejudice*, 319.

exclusively on his holiness even if you don't want to. Like Elizabeth and Mr. Darcy were with each other, you'll be better when you're involved with him.

So how do you do this? There are many ways; here are three:

First, pray for the courage to face God, to admit what you lack and to ask him to dwell in your heart.

John Donne wrote a poem that can be the foundation for just such a prayer. In one of his Holy Sonnets, he implored:

> Batter my heart, three-person'd God, for you
> As yet but knock, breathe, shine and seek to mend;
> That I may rise and stand, o'erthrow me, and bend
> Your force to break, blow, burn and make me new.[6]

He wanted God to take the lead because his own heart and mind weren't strong enough to do it:

> I, like a usurp'd town to another due
> Labor to admit you, but oh, to no end;
> Reason, your viceroy in me, me should defend
> But is captiv'd, and proves weak or untrue.[7]

Reason . . . proves weak and untrue. Don't try to figure him out or think your way into a relationship with him; just pray. Ask God to batter your heart; seek his help and wrestle with him to obtain his blessing like Jacob did. There's no better way for him to reverse the course of your nature. It takes courage but it also may be a relief; you can unburden yourself by asking him to take the lead and do what you can't do by yourself.

And remember also, how he answers your prayer is up to him. Don't be discouraged if you don't instantly feel like you're in a relationship with him; like Mr. Darcy you may find yourself in the middle before you know you've begun.

---

6. Donne, "Batter My Heart," 126.
7. Donne, "Batter My Heart," 126.

* * *

Second, listen to him and let him awaken your conscience so you can do his will.

Start with the Bible.

You may have already read a few things about him. You may know, for example, that his Ten Commandments and Sermon on the Mount teach us how to behave; that he performs miracles, like parting the Red Sea and walking on water; and that he is powerful, creating the universe and smiting empires. It's important to know all of these things about him and more, and they're all worth studying. But for present purposes there's one more thing about God that you should know. It's very important but frequently overlooked. And that is, he knows you.

It's easily forgotten because his teachings fill our sermons and the stories of his miraculous and powerful works seize our attention. And we also forget that he knows us because when God does get personal, he often does big things through famous people, people with whom we seem to have little in common (or at least these are the stories we remember).

We know about Abraham for instance. God provided for him and he grew wealthy; God told him "I am your shield," and he battled kings (Gen 15:1 NIV); God promised him "I will make you into a great nation," and he became the patriarch of Israel (Gen 12:2 NIV); God told him to "count the stars . . . so shall your offspring be," even though he and his wife Sarah were childless (Gen 15:5 NIV); and of course God established his covenant through him.

Abraham was a man full of faith and the Bible says he was blameless; he was the father of a nation and the recipient of God's covenant; he was someone with whom God had a personal relationship—and he was someone who seems so unlike us.

Abraham, however, isn't the prototype.

Think about Jacob and Peter. Each had a personal relationship with God and accomplished great things; Jacob was a descendant of Abraham and fulfilled God's covenant, and Peter was a disciple of

Jesus who led God's church. But Jacob was also a temperamental and scheming man who wrestled with God, and Peter was a zealous man who denied Jesus three times in a matter of hours.

They accomplished great things but they were hardly blameless.

God also spoke to his prophet Jeremiah and he was not only flawed; he failed accomplish what he set out to do. God told him to "speak to all the people . . . [so they will] listen and . . . turn from their evil ways" (Jer 26:3 NIV). Otherwise God would make their land "a curse among all the nations" (Jer 26:6 NIV). So Jeremiah told the nation of Israel that it should surrender to Nebuchadnezzar and submit to Babylon in order to survive and, at the same time, atone for their sins against God.

Jeremiah heard the word of God and shared it with the people of Israel. And what did he accomplish? King Zedekiah rejected the prophecy; the people threw Jeremiah into a cistern; and the army of Babylon burned Jerusalem, demolished the temple and took the people into exile. It all unfolded just as Jeremiah had warned.

Jeremiah was rescued but the futility of his life's work embittered him. His lamentations were a large part of his story and they included his accusation against God, that "you deceived me Lord, and I was deceived; you overpowered me and prevailed" (Jer 20:7 NIV).

Decades after he died the exiles returned home to Israel to receive a new covenant; this was also part of Jeremiah's prophecy. In his lifetime, however, his message was thoroughly rejected.

He is remembered as "the weeping prophet."

So we see that God talks to people who were far from blameless and who failed in their missions. In the New Testament the story continues as God talks to common people from all walks of life. We see Jesus mixing with tax collectors and priests; a wedding party and a prostitute; children and soldiers; and a rich young man and a poor old widow.

As we said earlier Abraham isn't the prototype; there is no prototype.

* * *

Listen for God but don't expect to hear him thunder. He may not want you to found a nation and call it to repent. If you think of yourself as an ordinary person you're no less important to him. Your conversations with him may be private and end with you:

> And when you pray, do not be like the hypocrites, for they love to pray standing in the synagogues and on the street corners to be seen by others. . . . But when you pray, go into your room, close the door, and pray to your Father, who is unseen. Then you Father, who sees what you've done in secret, will reward you (Matt 6:5–7).

He rejects melodrama and phony theatrics; there's a modest side to this carpenter who was born in a manger. "A quiet conscience," Anne Frank wrote, "makes one strong."[8] He probably would have agreed.

* * *

And he isn't above feeling an emotional attachment with you, one that also begins and ends with you. His relationship with Lazarus is a case in point.

We know very little about Lazarus except that he was a friend and follower of Jesus and that when he became ill, messengers went to Jesus and told Him that "the one you love is sick" (John 11:3 NIV). He travelled back to the town where Lazarus was but by the time he arrived, Lazarus was dead. And when Jesus saw the tomb of his friend, he—God himself—wept.

Even a sparrow doesn't fall to the ground "outside your Father's care," he told us in the Sermon on the Mount (Matt 10:29 NIV). "So don't be afraid; you are worth more than many sparrows" (Matt 10:31 NIV).

Likewise he isn't above wanting to know what you think. In a few telling instances the Bible emphasizes that he can get

---

8. Frank, *The Diary*, 707.

quite close to you. When "the teachers of the law" thought Jesus blasphemed by using his authority to forgive sin, for example, the Bible says that Jesus, "knowing their thoughts," reproached them (Matt 9:3–4 NIV).

He knows us. "The very hairs of your head are all numbered," he said (Matt 10:30 NIV).

It all matters; he sweats the small stuff.

If you want him to be involved in your life and to develop the chemistry through which he can save you, listen for him. And listen closely; he might speak to you in a whisper.

* * *

Third, harkening back to Einstein, pause to wonder and stand wrapped in awe.

Einstein referred to what he called the "miraculous order" in the universe; he saw evidence for God in the way the laws of physics hold everything together and make everything work. And we, too, can see evidence for him in the natural world, maybe in a beautiful sunset, a snowcapped mountain or how vegetation comes to life in springtime. But there's also evidence for God in some very unlikely places, especially where man's involved.

Imagine a desolate landscape, say a vast and windswept desert. Maybe you see a harsh and lifeless environment, one in which God couldn't possibly take an interest or manifest his presence. A poet like William Blake, however, could imagine him there, and he could express it in just a few lines. Thousands of years after the exodus, he wrote a stanza about a tribe of misfits wandering under the blinding sun and trudging through the burning sands of the Sinai. He wrote that:

> The Atoms of Democritus
> And Newton's Particles of Light
> Are sands upon the Red Sea shore,
> Where Israel's tents do shine so bright.[9]

---

9. Blake, "Mock On," 382.

The physical characteristics of the desert—those atoms and particles—were more than arid sand and blinding light; they were the stage for a trial of God's Chosen People, a harsh and essential condition for an act of penance on the way to the Promised Land.

Like Einstein said, there's a spirit manifest in the laws of the universe. It may not be pleasant but it's always meaningful. Be curious and look around you.

There's also evidence for God in how he affects us individually. We've seen him at work, for example, when Nicholai Bukharin's feelings of sympathy battled his fidelity to communism. It was an especially historic and dramatic instance of him working on one man's conscience, but of course Bukharin isn't the only person whose beliefs and actions he's tried to influence. We, too, hear his voice every day.

We may forget about it, wrestle with it or obey it, but however we deal with him we tend to do so in private; we usually don't share what he's telling us with our family and friends. But don't doubt for a moment that these battles are every bit as important as Bukharin's. George Eliot was right that . . .

> . . . the growing good of the world is partly dependent on unhistoric acts; and that things are not so ill with you and me as they might have been, is half owing to the number who lived faithfully a hidden life, and rest in unvisited tombs.[10]

He works on us even when nobody notices, and it matters.

Evidence for God abounds in the natural world and in human nature. Hugo of Saint Victor summed it up in one sentence. "All nature," he wrote, "speaks God."[11]

* * *

---

10. Eliot, *Middlemarch*, 640.
11. Cizewski, "Reading The World," 67.

We should raise a few caution flags, however, about how far studying the Bible and his creation can take us; our expectations should be in the right place.

First, reading about God, or seeing evidence for him within and around us, can bring us closer to him but that doesn't mean that we can comprehend him or figure him out entirely.

Nowadays it's hard for us to accept that limitation. We prefer to think that we know more than we do because we live in an era in which information is plentiful and readily available, and technological innovations and discoveries unfold at a dizzying pace. We can figure out so much; it's only natural to think that we can figure him out too.

It's hard to say where this will lead us but the past may offer a clue. There were other times in human history when the pace of learning suddenly accelerated by leaps and bounds. How it affected our ancestors' religious lives may tell us something about where we're going.

The Renaissance of the 1400s and 1500s, as one example, was an era that was similar to ours. It was when Christopher Columbus sailed to the New World and Leonardo Davinci drew pictures of flying machines and parachutes; Andreas Vesalius mapped human anatomy and Copernicus mapped the solar system; and the printing press put these and countless other theories and discoveries into books, which were more commonly available than at any previous time in human history. And so it seemed to the people of the fifteenth and sixteenth centuries, like it does to us in the twenty-first century, that there was nothing man can't figure out.

The spirit of their times had quite an effect on how they learned about God and the world around them. The Catholic monk Erasmus exaggerated (but only a little) when he wrote about his interest in Greek literature, "The first thing I shall do, as soon as the money arrives, is to buy some Greek authors; after that, I shall buy clothes."[12] The Protestant reformer Martin Luther taught at the University of Wittenberg and rejected any church dogma that he thought had no foundation in the Bible.

---

12. Corrigan and Schoeck, *The Collected Works*, 252.

Instead, he encouraged his students to engage their minds and study their bibles to understand their faith, all unfiltered by the history and hierarchy of the Catholic church. He echoed the rallying cry of his colleagues—*ad fontes!* (back to the source!)—so his students could go right to scripture with only their reason (and Luther) to guide them through it.

Erasmus and Luther were both brilliant thinkers. They studied the Bible; they read theologians like Augustine and Aquinas; and they were conversant in the history and doctrines of the church. They even shared similar views on some of the problems within it. Yet as their relationship grew it also became clear that they thought differently about God; in fact, each was sure that the other was dead wrong about his faith. And that's where their troubles began. From the common ground of intense study and learning grew two mighty trees whose roots and branches became entangled with each other, fighting for sovereignty over the soil.

They mostly argued about whether salvation came through faith in God or man's good deeds. Luther was certain that faith in God saved man, and he found most of his answers by interpreting the Bible; Erasmus was certain that man's good deeds saved him, and he found most of his answers by interpreting his creation. This debate over the salvation of man was one of their legacies, but the way they went about it left a dubious legacy as well.

Luther spared no words in his condemnation of Erasmus. "Whenever I pray," Luther wrote, "I pray for a curse upon Erasmus"[13] who was "the vilest miscreant who ever disgraced the earth"[14] and "the worst enemy that Christ had in a thousand years."[15] Erasmus mocked and insulted Luther's pride in return. "Dare Erasmus attack Luther," he asked, "like the fly the elephant?"[16] Their arguments degenerated into personal attacks that, in bitterness and malice, were the forerunners of the religious

---

13. Hazlitt, *Table Talk*, 283.
14. Hazlitt, *Table Talk*, 283.
15. Russell, *Library Notes*, 309.
16. Rupp and Watson, *Luther and Erasmus*, 36.

wars between Catholics and Protestants, and among various Protestant sects, in the 1600s and 1700s.

Shakespeare was a product of The Renaissance too and he absorbed much of what it had to offer; he certainly had no problem learning at an accelerated pace. But he went in a different direction. In spite of the times in which he wrote, he knew that there were limits to what man could know. He was particularly concerned that his contemporaries were becoming infatuated with reason and that they were trying to comprehend things that were fundamentally mysterious, like the key to salvation and the nature of God himself.

There are a couple of scenes in *Hamlet* where Shakespeare is especially effective at getting his point across. In one of them, Hamlet sets out to exact revenge on Claudius, the man who killed his father. And he wants to do more than transfix him with a sword. Since Hamlet's father was suffering in purgatory, he wants his murderer to suffer in time *and* eternity; he wants to send him to Hell. But when Hamlet finds Claudius alone and vulnerable but kneeling in prayer, he suddenly hesitates; as long as he is communing with God, Hamlet thinks, he is "fit and seasoned for his passage" to Heaven.[17] If he'd killed Claudius then and there, it would have been "hire and salary, not revenge."[18] So Hamlet leaves him alone and waits for another opportunity.

Hamlet thought that he knew how to determine the destiny of Claudius' soul. It turned out, however, that he knew nothing of the sort. After Hamlet left, Claudius got off his knees and said that God didn't hear his prayer because it was insincere. "My words fly up," Claudius said, "my thoughts remain below; words without thoughts never to heaven go."[19]

And in another scene we see Hamlet talking to his friend, the scholar Horatio. He was a student of philosophy and a man of his times, one whose type you could've found all over England and Europe, especially in the universities; these "humanists" believed

17. Hamlet (Bullen), 3.3.85.
18. Hamlet (Bullen), 3.3.78.
19. Hamlet Bullen), 96–97,

that man could discover the truth about anything by reasoning carefully and applying logic. But Hamlet took issue with all of it; he cautioned Horatio that reason alone couldn't explain what was rotten in the state of Denmark. He thought the answer ran much deeper. "There are more things in heaven and earth," he told him, "than are dreamt of in your philosophy."[20]

We should read the Bible and study creation to draw closer to God, experience his presence and be awed by the mystery. There are things that we can know about him and dispute in good faith, but we shouldn't try to figure him out entirely or attack those with different opinions about the most nuanced and difficult mysteries that he presents.

In Psalm 46, God speaks against all of the strife and violence in the world, including the schisms among believers. "Be still," he says, "and know that I am God" (Ps 46:10 NIV). It's commonly quoted as a piece of advice, a simple admonition to slow down so we can hear his voice. And as such it's a useful verse to remember. But it's also more than that; in Psalm 46 it is God's command, one that he issues —and enforces—against armies that are at war. "He lifts his voice," the psalm says, and "the earth melts" (Ps 46:6 NIV).

It makes you wonder whether Erasmus or Luther ever read that passage.

Look for evidence of God, draw closer to him and learn all that you can about him; but don't narrowly define him or try to comprehend who he is. If you do, you'll turn friends into enemies and neglect him along the way.

* * *

Second, it's important to remember that, while his creation includes evidence for him and his goodness, it also includes evils that are repugnant to his nature. We know why this is so; we know what happened when Adam and Eve divorced themselves from him; he expelled them from Eden, he took a step back and his creation unraveled a bit. As a result we've all had to live with the world's

---

20. Hamlet (Bullen), 1.5.165–166.

thorns and thistles, and when we look for him in these parts of the world that are our creation, we should keep in mind that they're a reflection of our nature, not his.

The English clergyman William Paley famously supported his belief in God by drawing an obvious inference from a simple metaphor; he said that the universe runs like a watch, which implies the existence of a watchmaker. It's the argument for God based on intelligent design or natural theology, and it's not a bad argument except for one fact, and it's a big and bracing fact; things go wrong in the world, sometimes terribly wrong. So if the universe is a watch, it operates like its springs have gotten a little rusty and its crystal has gotten a few scratches.

Does this imply that God doesn't exist? No; it's just the result of man taking the watch from God and placing it on his own wrist. Fortunately the Watchmaker didn't close shop and leave town so his invention still functions well enough that we can imagine how it operated when he alone was keeping time.

Third, when we do encounter evidence for his goodness in creation, we should be mindful that, as much as we admire it, creation (or any part of it) isn't God. He stands apart from his handiwork. And here we need to circle back to Einstein, who sometimes confused the two. Why he might have done so holds a valuable lesson for us.

It's true that sometimes Einstein sounded like an evangelical minister, rhapsodizing about the "music of the spheres," taking on "fanatical atheists" and sensing a "subtle, intangible and inexplicable" "spirit" in the universe that made it a "miraculous order"; and he did say that he venerated a "force" that was "behind anything that can be experienced" and "behind all discernible laws and connections," suggesting that he believed in an unmoved mover that was separate from creation. But other times it seemed like he believed that God and one part of his creation—physics—had merged into one being; he said, for example, that he reserved his "unbounded admiration" only for the "structure of the world as far as our science can reveal it."[21] Taken as a whole, his expressions of faith were a bit of a muddle.

This much is clear, however; although Einstein believed in God, he said "I do not believe in a personal God," and we should take him at his word.[22] This is understandable. He was a physicist, not a theologian; he studied the cosmos, not the Bible. He didn't produce an exegesis of the old and new testaments, and in any event turning to him for an opinion on the God of the Bible would be as foolish as turning to a preacher for an analysis of quantum mechanics.

To the extent he thought about a Creator at all, it seems like Einstein the believer marched up the hill but Einstein the physicist marched back down again. Theology has a lot of nuances so we may never know what Einstein truly believed, maybe because he didn't know what he truly believed. All we can say is that, as a physicist, it certainly made sense for him to try to get the heavens into his head but, as a believer, he may have been better served trying to get his head into the heavens.

When Einstein suggested that the science of physics was the god he venerated, it may have been his pride talking. We all can be led by our pride and Einstein was human after all, so he was no exception. Intellectuals can be proud too, and scientists in particular can be especially proud of their theories; like parents who have outsized expectations for their children, they sometimes see more in their theories than is there. "There's nothing my baby can't do!" So like Darwin, who thought evolution explained morality, Einstein seemed to believe, sometimes at least, that physics itself was God and that his theories were demigods.

If Einstein looked upon his theories the way a proud parent looks upon his children, his delight in them is understandable and easily forgiven; he certainly produced some overachievers. What's important for our purposes is that, while we can forgive a savant for being wrapped up in his genius, we have no such excuse for ourselves. Whatever we may do for a living, most of us aren't slaves

21. Overbye, "Einstein Letter," 9.
22. Dukas, *Albert Einstein*, 43.

to our genius and there's no reason for us to magnify the importance of our daily grind. We shouldn't deify, or act as if we're worshipping the little corner of his creation where we work or excel; remember, he's a jealous God.

We should take time away from our work and allow ourselves to pause in wonder and stand wrapped in awe at the incomprehensible scope of his creation. If nothing else it'll humble us; it'll remind us that some of his creation may fit in our heads, and more than a little if we're geniuses, but nowhere near all of it.

Which is another way of saying that most of us, thankfully, have time for the Sabbath.

* * *

"The Sabbath was made for man," he told us, "not man for the Sabbath" (Mark 2:27 NIV).

God rested on the seventh day and reflected on the goodness of his creation but he continued to be present in the lives of his people; and Jesus gathered grain and healed a man's withered hand on the Sabbath. We see by his example that he gave us the Sabbath to enjoy his creation and care for each other. It's a time for us to rest from regular work, but we don't sleep through it.

"The heavens declare the glory of God," says the psalmist, "the skies proclaim the work of his hands" (Ps 19:1 NIV). Leave your daily grind behind and pause to wonder and stand wrapped in awe; spend some time looking for signs of him. Science reveals God's goodness and wisdom; true love originates in him; pride explains our suffering; suffering can perfect us in a surprising way; the gifts that we give commemorate his gift of salvation—and on the Sabbath we have time to reflect upon it all, and refresh ourselves.

"Seek and you will find" (Matt 7:7 NIV). It's not as hard as you think; he isn't hiding. You can find his fingerprints "In the beginning . . ." and in evolution; in the dedication of the Hoover Dam and a meeting at home plate; in the lives and deaths of an industrialist, a clergyman, and two soldiers from World War II; in Stalin's show trials and Shakespeare's plays; in a magazine headline, a famous short story and an anecdote about an anonymous Sikh; in thoughtful gifts and . . . everything else that makes up the drama and comedy of life.

Notice too how he takes the lead in forming a bond with you. You pray, but he opens your heart; you listen, but he speaks; you pause to wonder and stand wrapped in awe, but after all it is he who is awesome. If you want him to plant himself in your heart, you'll need faith to do your part. But don't despair; "If you have faith as small as a mustard seed," he told us, "you can say to this mountain, 'Move from here to there,' and it will move" (Matt 17:20 NIV).

That's especially true when it comes to starting a relationship with him, because he does the heavy lifting.

Bibliography

Alighieri, Dante. *The Divine Comedy, Volume I: Inferno*. Translated by Mark Musa. New York: Penguin, 2003.
Amis, Martin. *Koba The Dread*. New York: Hyperion, 2001.
———. "Martin Amis on Lenin's Deadly Revolution." *New York Times*, October 16, 2017. https://www.nytimes.com/2017/10/16/books/review/martin-amis-lenin-russian-revolution.html
Aquinas, Thomas. *Summa Theologica Part I-II: Pars Prima Secundae*. Munich: Jazzybee Verlag, 2012. EBook.
———. *The Three Greatest Prayers, Commentaries on The Our Father, The Hail Mary, and The Apostles' Creed*. Translated by Laurence Shapcote. London: Burns, Oates & Washbourne, 1937.
Austen, Jane. *Pride and Prejudice*. New York: Charles Scribner's Sons, 1918.
Barlow, Nora, ed. *The Autobiography of Charles Darwin 1809-1882*. London: Collins, 1958.
Basler, Roy P, ed. *The Collected Works of Abraham Lincoln*. Vol. 2, New Brunswick: Rutgers University Press, 1953.
BBC News. "Islamic State Issues 'al-Baghdadi Message.'" May 14, 2015. https://www.bbc.com/news/world-middle-east-32744070
Blake, William. "Mock On, Mock On, Voltaire, Rousseau." In *The Top 500 Poems*, edited by William Harmon, 382. New York: Columbia University Press, 1992.
Bonney, Richard. *Jihād: from Qur'ān to Bin Laden*. New York: Palgrave Macmillan, 2004.
Bukharin, Nicolai. "Moscow Trials. The Case of Bukharin." https://www.marxists.org/archive/bukharin/works/1938/trial/3.htm

BIBLIOGRAPHY

———. "1925-N I Bukharin: 'Enrich Yourselves,' Excerpt from a report to a conference of Moscow party activists: 'On the new economic policy and our tasks.'" http://www.korolevperevody.co.uk/obogashchaytes.html

Bukharin, Nicolai, and E. Preobrazhensky. "The ABC of Communism." https://www.marxists.org/archive/bukharin/works/1920/abc/11.htm

Bureau of Reclamation. "The Story of Hoover dam – Essays: Artwork." March 12, 2015. https://www.usbr.gov/lc/hooverdam/history/essays/artwork.html.

Burleigh, Michael and Wolfgang Wippermann. *The Racial State: Germany 1933-1945*. New York: Cambridge University Press, 1991.

Burlingame, Michael. *Abraham Lincoln: A Life, Volume One*. Baltimor: The Johns Hopkins University Press, 2008.

Calaprice, Alice. *The Einstein Almanac*. Baltimore: JHU Press, 2005.

Caspar, Max. *Kepler*. Translated by C. Doris Hellman. New York: Dover, 1993.

Caute, David. *The Left In Europe Since 1789*. New York: McGraw-Hill, 1966.

Chambers, Whittaker. Introduction to *Witness*, by Whittaker Chambers, xxxiii-l. Washington D.C.: Regnery, 2014.

Chesterton, G.K. *Orthodoxy*. New York: John Lane, 1909.

Cizewski, Wanda. "Reading The World As Scripture: Hugo Of St. Victor's *De Tribus Diebus*." *Florilegium* 9 (1987): 67. https://journals.lib.unb.ca

Corrigan, Beatrice and Richard J Schoeck, eds. *The Collected Works of Erasmus: The Correspondence of Erasmus*. Toronto: University of Toronto Press, 1974.

Curry, Oliver Scott. "Morality as Cooperation: A Problem-Centered Approach." In *The Evolution of Morality*, edited by T.K. Shackelford et. al, 27-51. New York: Springer International (2016)

Curry, Oliver Scott; Mullins, Daniel Austin; and Whitehouse, Harvey. "Is It Good To Cooperate? Testing the theory of morality-as-cooperation in 60 societies." *Current Anthropology* 60 (2019) 47-69.

Dābiq. "Just Terror." November 18, 2015.

Darwin, Charles. *The Descent of Man and Selection in Relation to Sex*. London: John Murray, 1871.

———. *Origin of the Species*. New York: P F Collier & Son, 1909.

Darwin, Francis, ed. *Charles Darwin: His Life Told In An Autobiographical Chapter, And In A Selected Series Of His Published Letters*. London: John Murray, 1892.

———. *The Life and Letters of Charles Darwin, including an autobiographical chapter*. Vol. 1. London: John Murray, 1887.

Dawkins, Richard. *Heart of the Matter: God Under the Microscope*. BBC, 1996. http://www.youtube.com/watch?v=2gTYFolrpNU&t=08m42s

———. "The Future Looks Bright." *The Guardian*. (June 2003) https://www.theguardian.com/books/2003/jun/21/society.richarddawkins.

———. "Why Darwin Matters." *The Guardian*. (February 2008) https://www.theguardian.com/science/2008/feb/09/darwin.dawkins1

BIBLIOGRAPHY

De Beer, Sir Gavin, ed. *Darwin's Notebooks on Transmutation of Species. Part II, Second Notebook.* Bulletin of the British Museum (Natural History) Historical Series, Vol. 2 no. 3. London: 1960.

de Tocqueville, Alexis. *Democracy in America*. Translated by Henry Reeve. New York: Bantam Dell, 2002.

Donne, John. "Batter My Heart, Three Personed God." In *The Top 500 Poems*, edited by William Harmon, 126. New York: Columbia University Press, 1992.

———. "The Relic." In *The Top 500 Poems*, edited by William Harmon, 151-152. New York: Columbia University Press, 1992.

Dostoyevsky, Fyodor. *Great Short Stories of Fyodor Dostoyevsky*. Translated by H.V. Blavatsky. Sydney: ReadHowYouWant, 2008.

Dukas, Helen. *Albert Einstein, The Human Side*. Princeton: Princeton University Press, 1981.

Einstein, Albert. *Albert Einstein, The Human Side*. Princeton: Princeton University Press, 2013.

———. *Einstein on Cosmic Religion and Other Opinions and Aphorisms*. Mineola, New York: Dover, 2009.

———. *Religion and Science. New York Times* (November 1930) https://graphics8.nytimes.com/images/blogs/learning/pdf/2013/19301109Einstein.pdf

Elliot, George. *Middlemarch*. Orchard Park: Broadview, 2004.

Escot, Colin, et. al. *Hank Williams: The Biography*. New York: Little Brown, 2009. EBook.

Fest, Joachim C. *Hitler*. New York: Harcourt Brace Jovanovich, 1974.

Frank, Anne. *The Diary of Anne Frank, The Revised Critical Edition*. New York: Doubleday, 2003.

Fulghum, Robert. *All I Really Need To Know I Learned In Kindergarten, Uncommon Thoughts On Common Things*. New York: Random House, 2003.

Getty, J. Arch and Oleg Naumov. *The Road to Terror: Stalin and the Self-Destruction of the Bolsheviks, 1932-1939*. Translations by Benjamin Sher. New Haven: Yale University Press, 1999.

Goldstein, Gerry. "On a Long Ago Diamond, a Beginning and an End." *Providence Journal*, March 27, 2019. https://www.providencejournal.com/news/20190327/on-long-ago-diamond-beginning-and-end

Gray, Thomas. "Elegy Written in a Country Churchyard." In *The Top 500 Poems*, edited by William Harmon, 327-332. New York: Columbia University Press, 1992.

Gregorian, Vahe. "Buck O'Neil Was Left Out of the Hall of Fame Ten Years Ago, but His Response Still Inspires Us Today." *Kansas City Star*, February 26, 2016. https://www.kansascity.com/sports/spt-columns-blogs/vahe-gregorian/article62807672.html

Gregory, Paul. *Politics, Murder and Love in Stalin's Kremlin: The Story of Nicolai Bukharin and Anna Larina*. Stanford: Hoover, 2013.

Hazlitt, William, ed. *The Table Talk Of Martin Luther*. Translated by William Hazlitt. London: H.G. Bohn, 1856.

Henry, O. *Selected Stories of O. Henry*, New York: Barnes and Noble, 2003.

———. "The Gift of the Magi." https://americanenglish.state.gov/files/ae/resource_files/1-the_gift_of_the_magi_0.pdf

Hitler, Adolph. *Mein Kampf*. Boston: Houghton Mifflin, 1971.

Huisking, Charlie. "Buck O'Neil 'Changed My Life,' Says Filmmaker." *Herald-Tribune*, April 10, 2007. https://www.heraldtribune.com/article/LK/20070410/News/605208565/SH

Isaacson, Walter. "Einstein & Faith." *Time* (April 2007). http://content.time.com/time/subscriber/article/0,33009,1607298-1,00.html.

Jammer, Max. *Einstein and Religion: physics and theology*. Princeton: Princeton University Press, 2002.

Kaden, S. "ALS: The Other 'Tyrant' in Gehrig's Life." https://moregehrig.tripod.com/id3.html

Kashatus, William. *Lou Gehrig: A Biography*. Westport: Greenwood, 2004.

Khomeini, Ayatollah Ruhollah. "Islam is Not a Religion of Pacifists." In *The Theory and Practice of Islamic Terrorism: An Anthology*, edited by Marvin Perry, et.al., 29-32. New York: Palgrave Macmillan, 2008.

Krieger, Tara. "Eleanor Gehrig," https://sabr.org/bioproj/person/eleanor-gehrig/#sdendnote5osym

Landes, Richard. *Heaven on Earth: The Varieties of the Millennial Experience*. New York: Oxford University Press, 2011.

Laski, Harold. *Communism*. London: Frank Cass, 1968.

Lenin, Vladimir. "'Left Wing' Communism: An Infantile Disorder. An essential condition of the Bolsheviks' success." https://www.marxists.org/archive/lenin/works/1920/lwc/ch02.htm

———. *Little Lenin Library*. Vol. 7, *Religion*. New York: International Publishers, 1935.

———. "On the Significance of Militant Materialism." https://www.marxists.org/archive/lenin/works/1922/mar/12.htm

Levy, Alan. *Joe McCarthy: Architect of the Yankee Dynasty*. Jefferson: McFarland, 2005.

Lewis, C.S. *A Grief Observed*. New York: Harper Collins, 2001.

———. *The C.S. Lewis Signature Classics*. New York: Harper One, 2017.

Liebich, André. "'I Am the Last'-Memories of Bukharin in Paris." *Slavic Review* 51, no. 4 (1992): 767-81. Accessed July 12, 2021. doi:10.2307/2500137.

Lucie-Smith, Fr. Alexander. "The Incredible Sacrifice of Salvo D'Acquisto." *Catholic Herald* (July 2012). https://catholicherald.co.uk/the-incredible-sacrifice-of-salvo-daquisto/

Mandelstam, Nadezha. *Hope Against Hope: A Memoir*. Translated by Max Hayward. London: Collins and Harvill, 1971.

Mandelstam, Osip. "Stalin Epigram." In *Breaking Free: An Anthology of Human Rights Poetry*, edited by Robert Hull, 47-52. Belmont: Thomson Learning, 1995.

BIBLIOGRAPHY

Martinez, Andy. "The Role Buck O'Neil Played in Ernie Banks Becoming 'Mr. Cub.'" https://www.marqueesportsnetwork.com/the-role-buck-oneil-played-in-ernie-banks-becoming-mr-cub/

Marx, Karl. "Private Property and Communism." https://www.marxists.org/archive/marx/works/1844/manuscripts/comm.htm

McKechnie, William Sharp. *Magna Carta, A Commentary on the Great Charter of King John*, Glasgow: James Maclehose and Sons, 1905.

McQueen, Alison. *The Rise of the Cult of Rembrandt: Reinventing an Old Master in Nineteenth Century France*. Amsterdam: Amsterdam University Press, 2003.

Midlarsky, Manus. *Origins of Political Extremism: Mass Violence in the Twentieth Century and Beyond*. New York: Cambridge University Press, 2011.

National Baseball Hall of Fame. "Luckiest Man." July 16, 2021. https://baseballhall.org/discover-more/stories/baseball-history/lou-gehrig-luckiest-man

National Baseball Hall of Fame. "Buck O'Neil – Baseball Hall of Fame Induction Ceremony Speech." YouTube Video, 7:25, January 18, 2012, https://www.youtube.com/watch?v=LtE2I6jsung

New York Times. "An Interview with Khomeini." October 7, 1979.

NPR. "Remembering Ernie Banks, A Fan Favorite Whose Favorite Was The Fans." https://www.npr.org/2015/01/24/379550432/remembering-ernie-banks-a-fan-favorite-whose-favorite-was-the-fans

NPR. "Wrigley Field, The Much Imitated, Never Duplicated Ballpark." https://www.npr.org/2014/05/24/315445184/wrigley-field-the-much-imitated-never-duplicated-ball-park

O'Neil, Buck. *I Was Right On Time, My Journey From The Negro Leagues To The Majors*. New York: Simon and Schuster, 1996.

Opie, I. and P. Opie, *The Oxford Dictionary of Nursery Rhymes*. London: Oxford University Press, 1951.

Overbye, Dennis. "Einstein Letter On God Sells For $404,000." *New York Times*, May 17, 2008. https://www.nytimes.com/2008/05/17/science/17einsteinw.html

Posnanski, Joe. "Joe Posnanski: Remembering 'Mr. Cub,' Ernie Banks." https://mlb.nbcsports.com/2015/01/24/joe-posnanski-remembering-mr-cub-ernie-banks/

———. "Buck." https://sportsworld.nbcsports.com/buck-oneil-joe-posnanski/

Preston, Diana. *Lusitania: An Epic Tragedy*. New York: Bloomsbury USA, 2015. EBook.

Radzinsky, Edward. *Stalin*. New York: Random House, 1997.

Raico, Ralph. *Great Wars and Great Leaders, A Libertarian Rebuttal*. Auburn: Ludwig Von Mises Institute, 2010.

Reis, Ronald. *Lou Gehrig*. New York: Checkmark, 2009.

Robinson, Ray. "Hall of Fame: Lou Gehrig, Columbia Legend and American Hero." In *Living Legacies at Columbia*, edited by Theodore de Bary et. al., 559-568. New York: Columbia University Press, 2006.

Rowe, David, and Robert Schulmann. *Einstein on Politics: His Private Thoughts and Public Stands on Nationalism*. Princeton: Princeton University Press, 2007.

Rupp, E. Gordon and Phillip S. Watson, eds. *Luther and Erasmus: Free Will and Salvation*. Translated by E. Gordon Rupp in collaboration with A.N. Marlow, and Phillip S. Watson in collaboration with B. Drewery. Louisville: Westminster John Knox, 2006.

Russell, Addison P. *Library Notes*. Boston: Houghton Mifflin, 1893.

Ryan, James. *Lenin's Terror: The Ideological Origins of Early Soviet State Violence*. New York: Routledge, 2012.

Salisbury, Harrison. "Bukharin and the Bolshevik Revolution." *New York Times*, November 25, 1973. https://www.nytimes.com/1973/11/25/archives/bukharin-and-the-bolshevik-revolution-by-stephen-f-cohen.html

Shakespeare, William. "Hamlet." In *William Shakespeare, The Complete Works*, edited by Arthur Henry Bullen, 670-713. New York: Dorset, 1988.

———. "Julius Caesar." In *William Shakespeare, The Complete Works*, edited by Arthur Henry Bullen, 582-610. New York: Dorset, 1988.

Shelley, Mary. *Frankenstein*. New York: Dover, 1994.

Thompson, Carlton. "O'Neil 'Probably the Greatest Ambassador of the Negro Leagues.'" https://www.mlb.com/history/negro-leagues/players/buck-oneil

Simon, Scott. "Let's Play Two! Remembering Chicago Cub Ernie Banks." https://www.npr.org/2015/01/24/379546360/lets-play-two-remembering-chicago-cub-ernie-banks

Sontheimer, Harald. *Diseases of the Nervous System*. London: Academic, 2021.

Stevenson, Burton. *Stevenson's Book of Quotations*. London: Cassell, 1948.

Trotsky, Leon. *Literature and Revolution*. Chicago: Haymarket Books, 2005.

———. "Antireligious Propaganda." *Pravda* (July 1924). https://thecharnelhouse.org/2015/01/02/bolshevik-antireligious-propaganda-part-ii-trotsky-and-the-red-army-prepare-to-storm-heaven/

Twain, Mark. *The Adventures of Huckleberry Finn*. Munich: GRIN Verlag, 2009.

Verducci, Tom. "A Different Kind Of Perfect." *Sports Illustrated*, June 14, 2010. https://vault.si.com/vault/2010/06/14/a-different-kind-of-perfect

visionaryproject. "John 'Buck' O'Neil: Beginning Of My Baseball Career." YouTube Video, 5:09, March 22, 2010, https://www.youtube.com/watch?v=N3FE-xZxzeQ

Ward, Geoffrey C., and Ken Burns. *Baseball, An Illustrated History*. New York: Alfred A. Knopf, 1994.

Wilson, Doug. *Let's Play Two: The Life and Times of Ernie Banks*. New York: Rowman and Littlefield, 2019.

Wright, Robin. *The Last Great Revolution: Turmoil and Transformation in Iran*. New York: Knopf Doubleday, 2010.

Young, Edward. *The Works of Edward Young*. London: Vernor and Hood, 1813.

www.ingramcontent.com/pod-product-compliance
Lightning Source LLC
Chambersburg PA
CBHW070915160426
43193CB00011B/1472